MANY KINDS OF ANIM[ALS]

Animals are living things. Some can fly in th[e air.] Many animals live on land. There are so ma[ny] different kinds of animals.

Among the many different kinds of animals in this book, you will see:

Mammals

Fish

Reptiles

Birds

Amphibians

Insects

Mollusks

There are even more kinds of animals, including ones that no longer live on the earth! Some of these, like the dinosaurs, can be found as you enjoy the pages of this book!

© School Zone Publishing 06338

ANIMAL HABITATS

Where an animal lives is called its **habitat**. Animals live in many different kinds of habitats all over the earth. The habitats shown in this book are:

Farm

City

Ocean

Desert

Arctic

Wetland

Forest

Savanna Grassland

River

Rain Forest

Prehistoric

An animal's natural habitat can provide it with food, shelter, protection, and other animals of its kind to start a family with.

These are just a few of the earth's habitats. Did you know that even your own home is a habitat for animals? What kinds of animals can you find living in your home?

RADIANT ROOSTER

Connect the dots from 1–20.
Color the picture.

COMPARABLE COWS

Draw a line from each calf to the cow that looks like it.

FARM FRIENDS

Find and circle the hidden pictures.

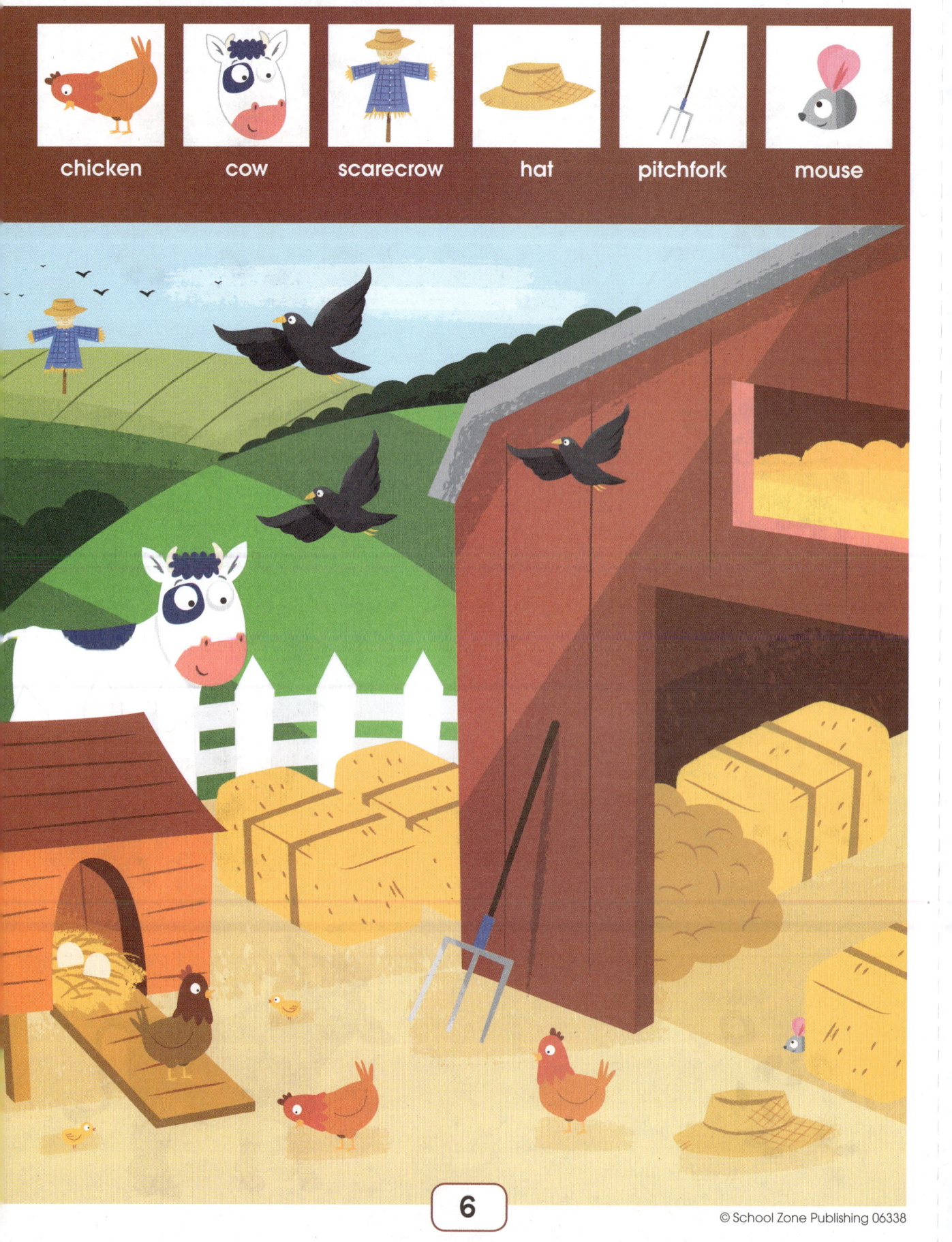

| chicken | cow | scarecrow | hat | pitchfork | mouse |

BARNYARD WORD SEARCH

Look at the word list.
Circle the words in the puzzle.

BEE   CAT   COW   DOG   FOX   PIG

A Y C A T I F G J
G Z R F P H B I O
E P I G H Y Q X K
H Z Q A F D O G V
D C P E J K L W I
F O X O R A D U J
M Z Q C U M B E E
K L B O N B T N C
C X T W E L D W V

HELLO, NELLIE!

Connect the dots from 1-20.
Color the picture.

FARMYARD FROLIC

Color one box for each animal you see in the picture below.

	1	2	3	4	5
Cows					
Sheep					
Chickens					
Goats					
Horses					

NAME THE ANIMALS

Write the beginning letter for each animal.

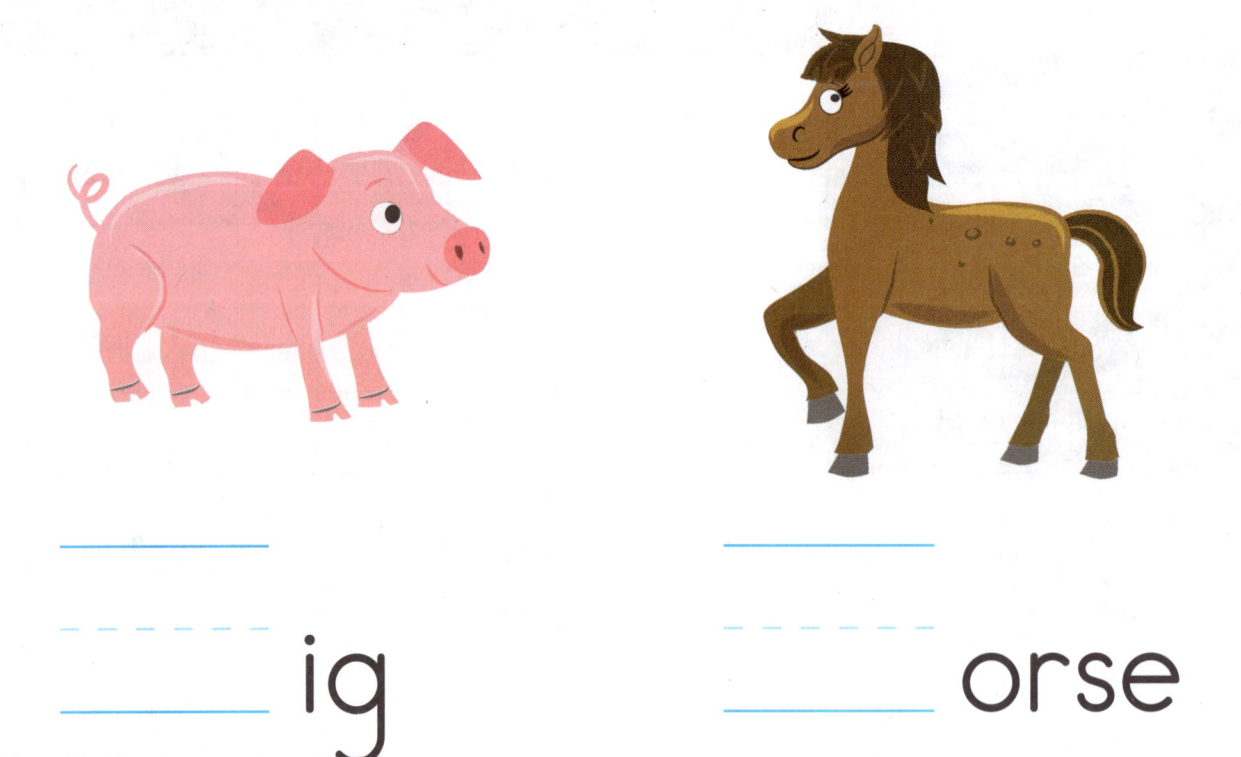

_____ ig

_____ orse

_____ oat

_____ ow

TWO LITTLE DUCKLINGS

Color the picture.

- ● = purple
- ● = green
- ● = yellow
- ● = orange
- ● = tan
- ● = blue

11

TO THE STABLES

Draw a line from the ➡ to the **End**.

End

BIG & LITTLE

Draw a line from each animal to the word that describes it.

BIG

SPOTTED

FAT

little

PIN THE TAILS

Draw a line from each animal's body to its tail.

15

A DAY ON THE FARM

Find and circle the hidden pictures.

| chick | pitchfork | mouse | spider | horseshoe | rope |

CHICKEN EGGS

Draw a line from each chicken to the egg that looks like it.

Color the eggs to complete the patterns.

17

WHAT'S DIFFERENT?

Find and circle **8** things that are different in **picture A** and **picture B**.

Picture A

Picture B

18

RIDDLE ME THIS

Solve the addition problems.
Use the code to solve the riddle below.

N
3 + 1 =

I
3 + 0 =

E
0 + 2 =

A
1 + 0 =

P
4 + 1 =

G
0 + 0 =

What does a pig use when he writes?

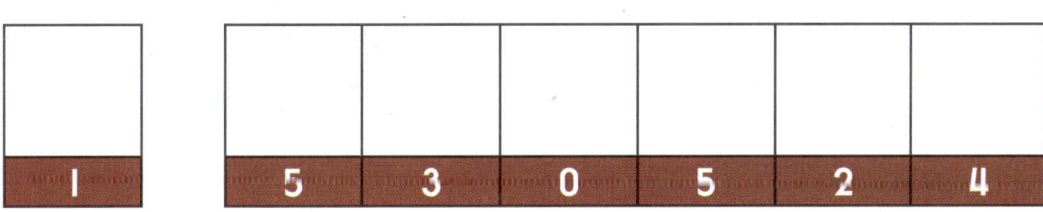

1	5	3	0	5	2	4

19

FARMER JACK'S FAVORITE

Read the clues to find the correct answer.

1. Farmer Jack's favorite animal has four legs.
2. His favorite animal has spots.
3. His favorite animal has gray fur.

Circle Farmer Jack's favorite animal.

FARMYARD CUTOUTS

Cut out the barn and animal pieces. Fold the paper on the lines to make the pieces stand up. Use the pieces to tell a story using the words **first**, **then**, **next**, and **last**.

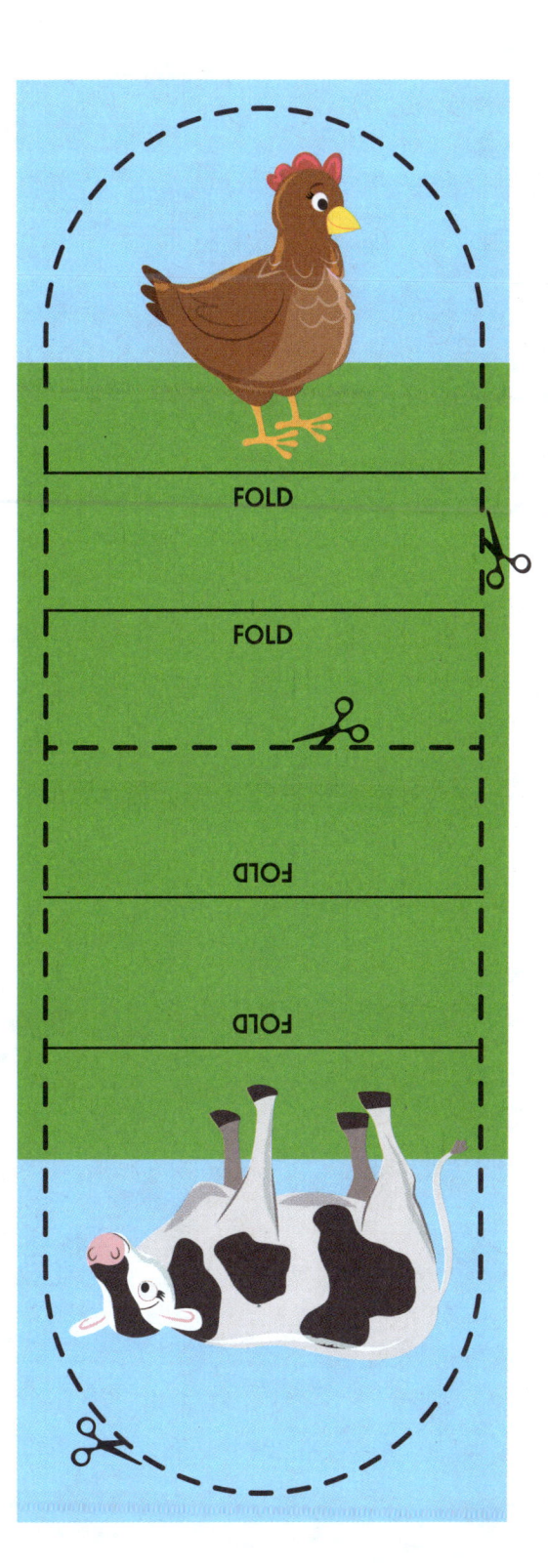

FOLD

FOLD

FOLD

FOLD

FOLD

FOLD

21

© School Zone Publishing 06338

COCK-A-DOODLE-DOO!

Cut out the puzzle pieces and mix them up.
Put the puzzle pieces together.

GEORGE'S FIELD DAY

Connect the dots from 1–20.
Color the picture.

25

LEARN TO DRAW

Step 1:
Draw the head.

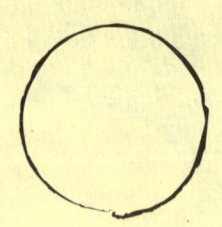

Step 2:
Draw the body and snout.

Follow the steps to draw pigs.

Step 3:
Draw the ears and legs.

Step 4:
Draw the face, toes, and tail.

TO THE BARN, BESSIE!

Draw a line from the ➡ to the **End**.

Color the hoof prints to complete the patterns.

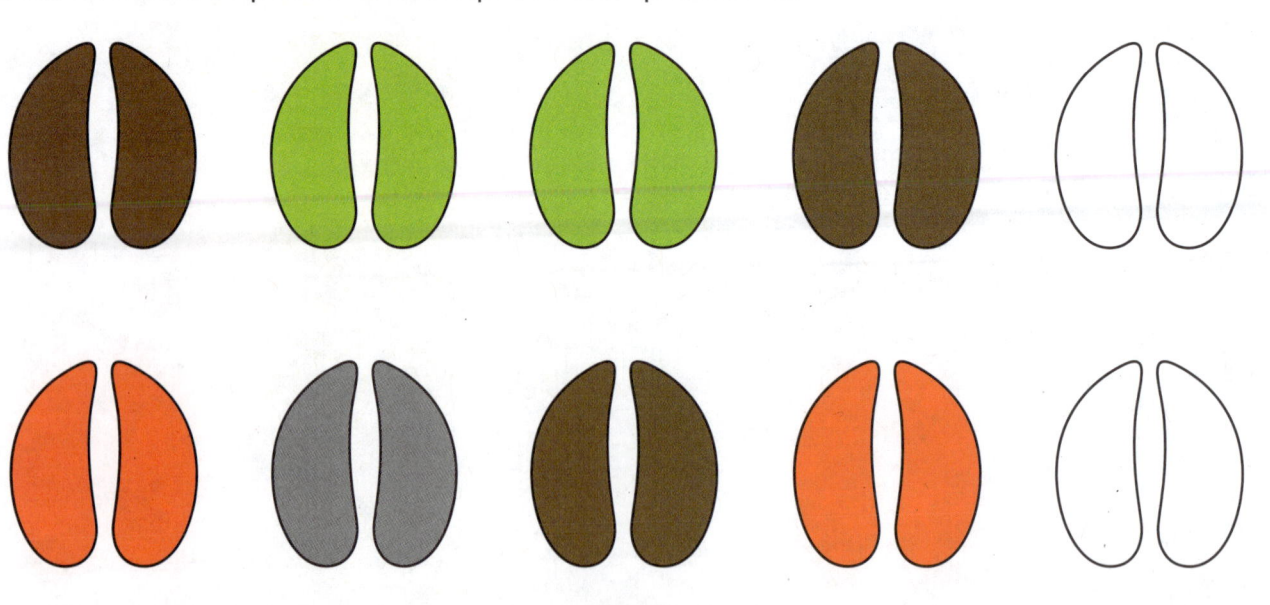

28

SPOTTED COWS

Trace each cow's spots. Color the picture.

ANIMAL SHADOWS

Draw a line from each animal to its shadow.

30

RIDDLE ME THIS

Solve the addition problems. Use the code to solve the riddle below.

R		S		H
0 + 1 =		1 + 2 =		1 + 3 =

A
2 + 0 =

O
3 + 2 =

E
0 + 0 =

Who always goes to bed with his shoes on?

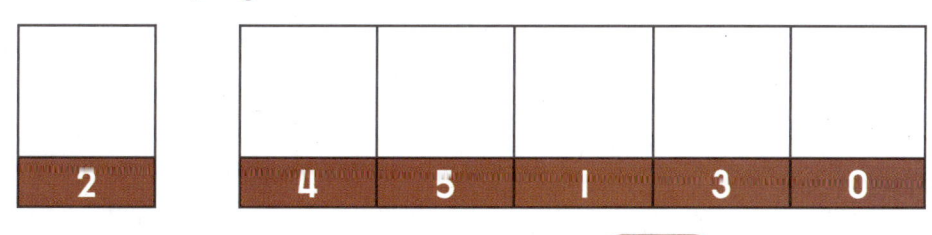

2	4	5	1	3	0

31

LEARN TO DRAW

Step 1:
Draw a **circle** for the head.

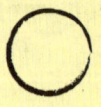

Step 2:
Draw a **half-circle** for the body.

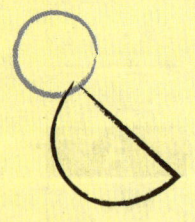

Follow the steps to draw chicks.

32

Step 3:
Draw a **triangle** for the beak and a line for the wing.

Step 4:
Draw a **dot** for the eye and lines for the legs and feathers.

33

APPLE ORCHARD

Draw a line from the ➡ to the **End**.

Color the pictures to complete the patterns.

FARM FRIENDS WORD SEARCH

Look at the word list.
Circle the words in the puzzle.

CAT   HEN   COW   DOG   DUCK   HORSE   GOOSE   PIG

```
S C H B M H E N M
D E O T W Y C Z P
U N R Q C P A V I
C H S E O A T L G
K C E U W P Z M X
V R Y I O Q D R M
J W F C G O O S E
M R B P R S Z F W
G O Y T G H D O G
```

35

NAME THE BIRDS

Write the beginning letter for each bird.

_____ awk

_____ uck

_____ oucan

_____ enguin

36

A DAY AT THE ZOO

Find the pictures below, and then check the box next to the picture.

☐ 1 stork   ☐ 1 emu    ☐ 3 penguins   ☐ 2 snowy owls

Color to complete the patterns.

37

NEW COLLARS

Draw a line from each dog to its collar.

38

BUSTER GOES OUTSIDE

Color the picture.

- ● = black
- ● = blue
- ● = pink
- ● = brown
- ● = green
- ● = dark green

39

BAMBOO FOR A PANDA

Connect the dots from 1-20.
Color the picture.

WHAT'S DIFFERENT?

Find and circle **6** things that are different in **picture A** and **picture B**.

Picture A

Picture B

41

ADDITION WITH PIGEONS

Fill in the numbers to finish the addition problems.

☐ + 3 = 5

1 + 1 = ☐

0 + ☐ = 2

5 + ☐ = 5

2 + 2 = ☐

☐ + 2 = 3

0 + ☐ = 1

1 + ☐ = 4

☐ + 0 = 3

1 + 0 = ☐

FRED'S DAY AT THE PARK

Cut out the puzzle pieces and mix them up.
Put the puzzle pieces together.

43

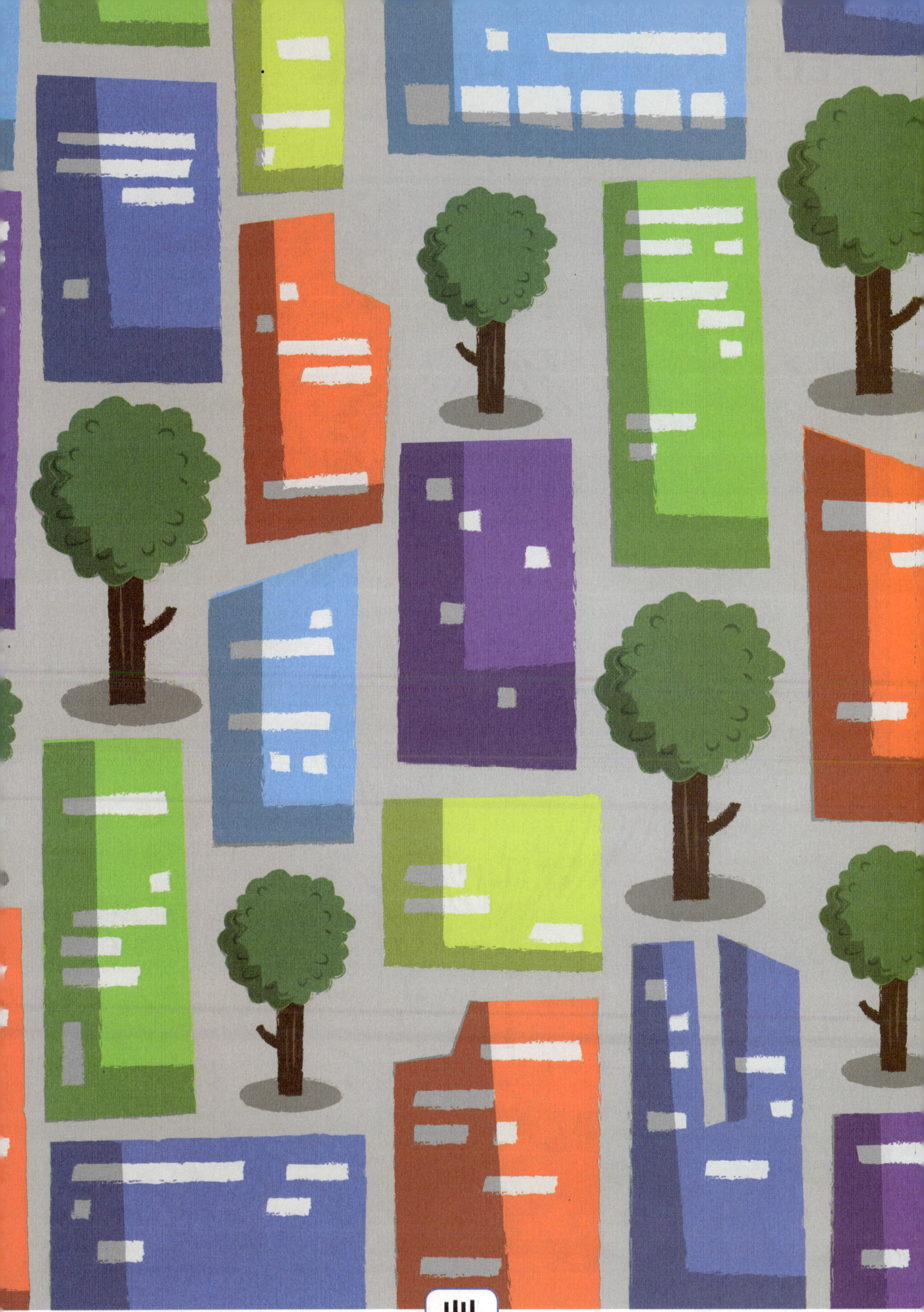

GIVE A DOG A BONE

Draw a line from the ➡ to the End.

Look at the pattern. Circle what comes next.

45

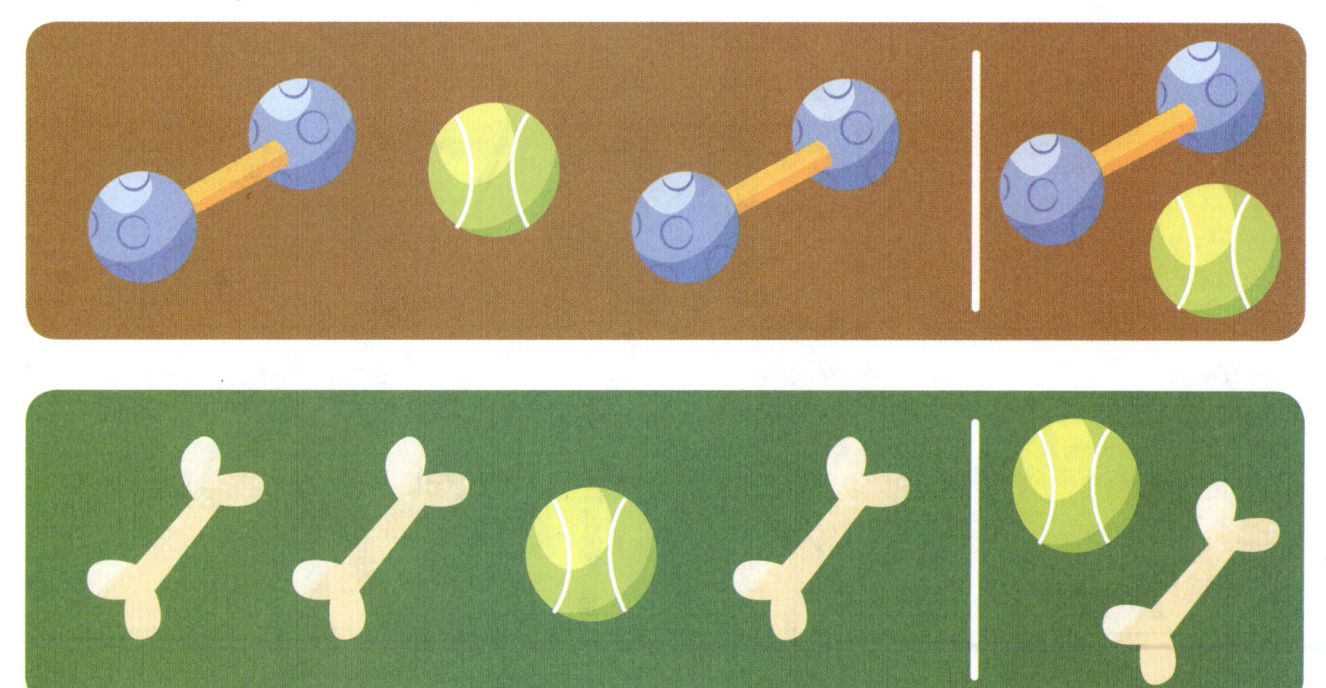

ZOO DAY!

Find and circle the hidden pictures.

| penguin | spider | lion | clown fish | flamingo | parrot | zebra |

CITY ANIMAL CUTOUTS

Cut out the city and animal pieces. Fold the paper on the lines to make the pieces stand up. Use the pieces to tell a story using the words **first**, **then**, **next**, and **last**.

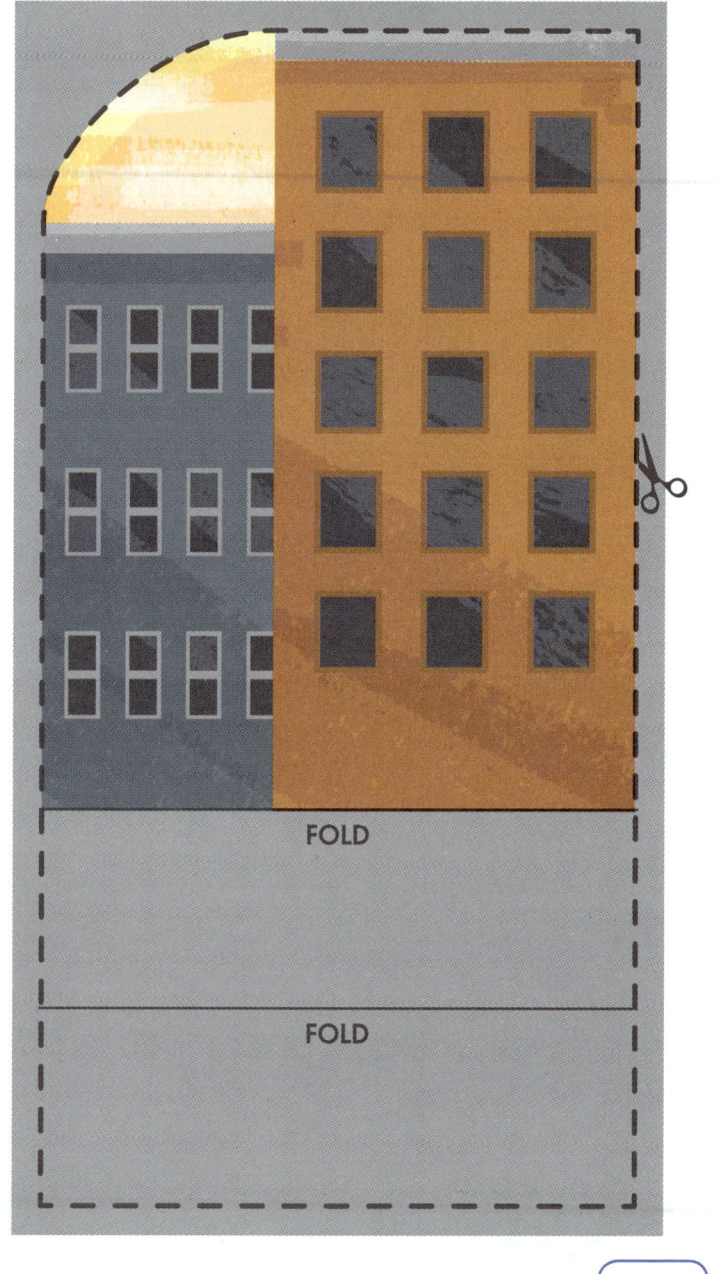

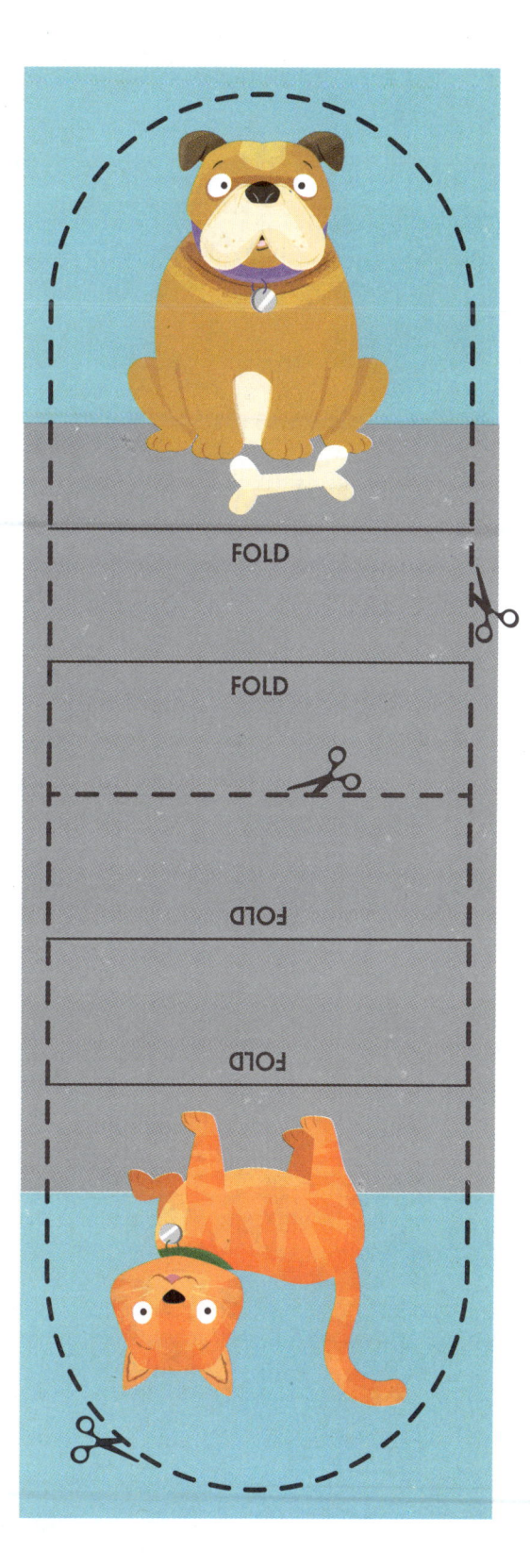

47

SNIFFING FOR BONES

Find and circle all of the 🦴's in the picture. How many did you find?

49

LEARN TO DRAW

Step 1:
Draw a **half-oval** for the body.

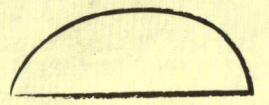

Step 2:
Draw **circles** for the ears.

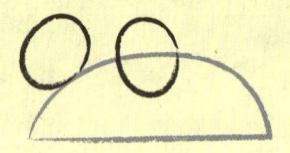

Step 3:
Draw the nose and eye.

Step 4:
Draw the whiskers and tail.

Step 1:
Draw a **circle** for the head.

Step 2:
Draw an **oval** for the body.

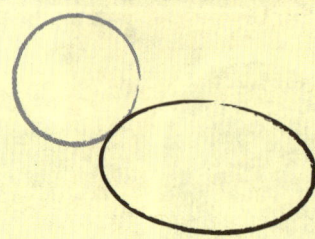

Step 3:
Draw the nose, ears, and legs.

Step 4:
Draw the eyes, whiskers, mouth, and tail.

Follow the steps to draw cats and mice.

51

GARDEN CRITTERS

Find the pictures below, and then check the box next to each picture.

☐ 1 snail

☐ 5 ants

☐ 4 butterflies

☐ 1 snake

☐ 3 ladybugs

☐ 5 bees

53

PIGEON'S STROLL

Color the picture.

- ● = green
- ● = gray
- ● = orange
- ● = pink
- ● = purple

54

PLAYTIME FOR WHISKERS

Connect the dots from 1–20.
Color the picture.

55

A CHEESY TREAT

Draw a line from the ➡ to the **End**.

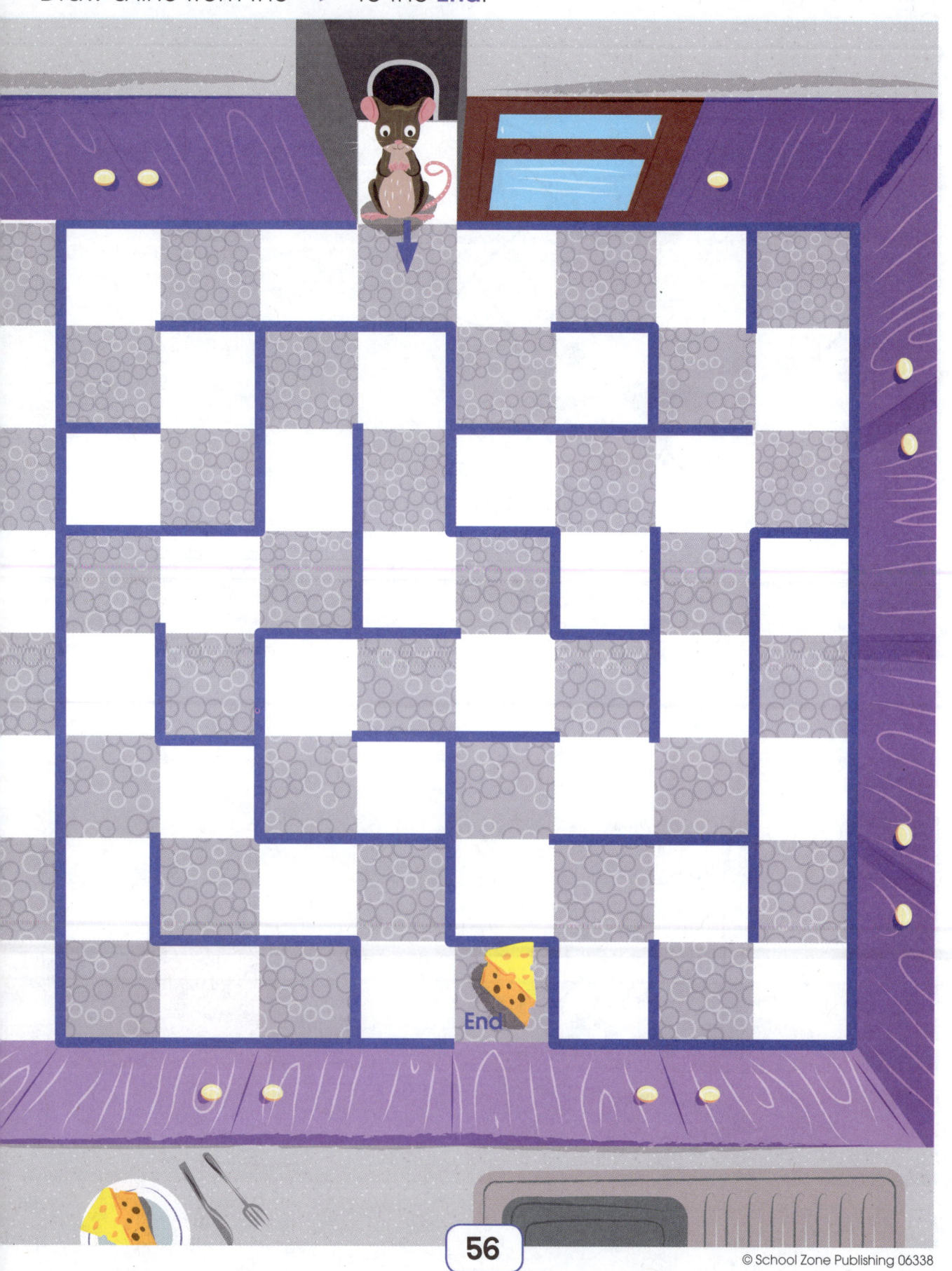

THE PET SHOP

Find and circle the hidden pictures.

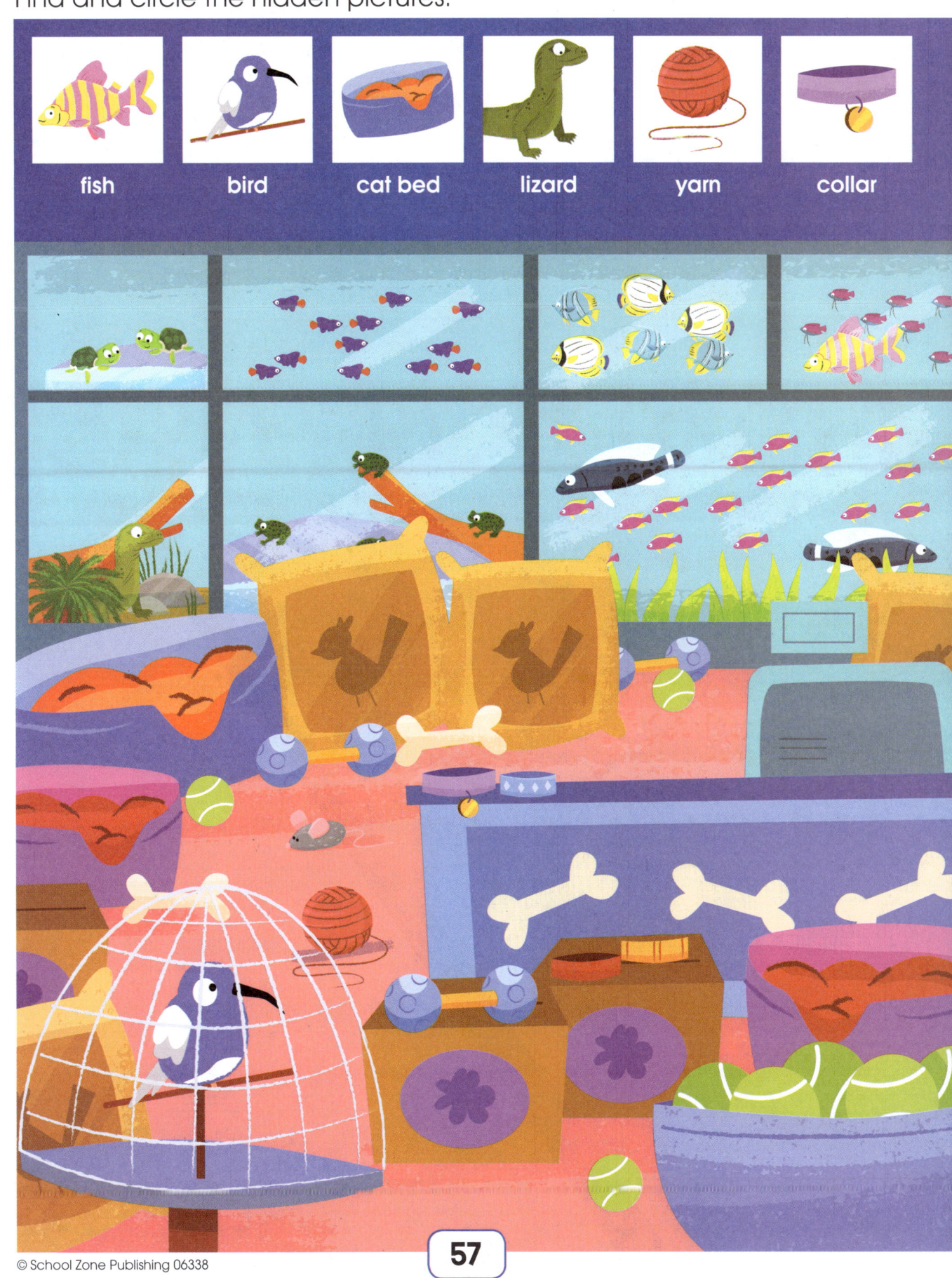

| fish | bird | cat bed | lizard | yarn | collar |

57

LEARN TO DRAW

Step 1:
Draw a **circle** for the head.

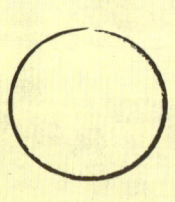

Step 2:
Draw another **circle** for the muzzle and an **oval** for the body.

Step 3:
Draw **triangles** for the nose and ears.

Step 4:
Draw **dots** for the eyes and lines for the mouth, tail, and legs.

Follow the steps to draw dogs.

59

PUPPY TREAT

Connect the dots from 1–20.
Color the picture.

60

BUZZING BEES

Find and circle all of the 🐝's in the picture. How many did you find?

TAME OR WILD?

Draw a line from each animal to the word that describes it.

tame
(An animal that is not dangerous or frightened of people. It may also be gentle enough to be kept as a pet.)

wild
(An animal that is not used to living around people or is dangerous. You might only see this kind of animal in a zoo.)

BUTTERFLY FRIEND

Cut out the puzzle pieces and mix them up.
Put the puzzle pieces together.

63

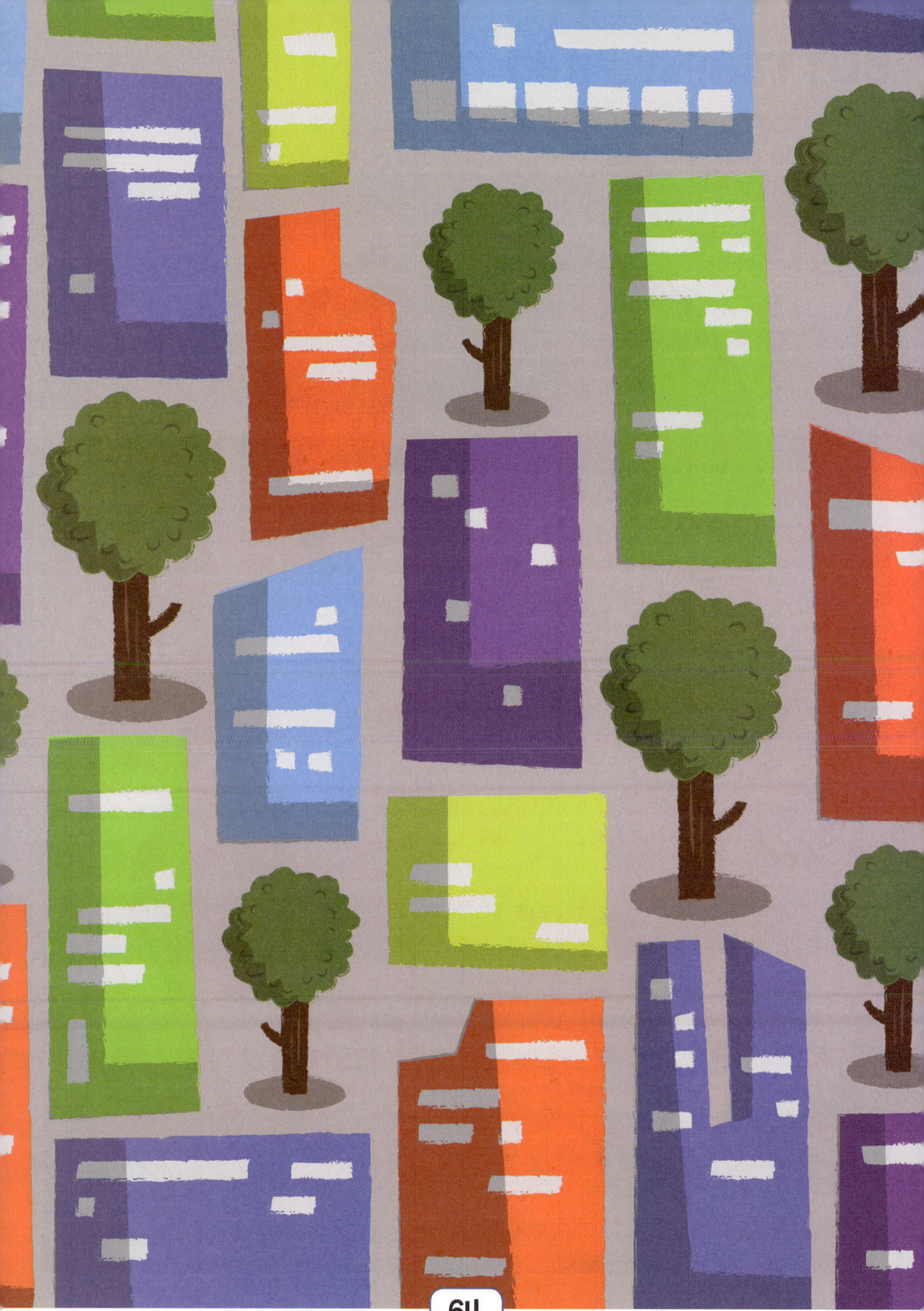

ANIMAL SOUNDS

Draw a line to match the animal to the sound it makes.

tweet-tweet

buzz

ribbit

woof-woof

meow

quack

65

GARDEN PARK

Find and circle the hidden pictures.

Find 1 rabbit

Find 2 toads

Find 4 snails

Find 4 butterflies

66

FOREST DEER

Connect the dots from 1-20.
Color the picture.

67

A HOPPING GOOD TIME

Find and circle all of the 🦗's in the picture. How many did you find?

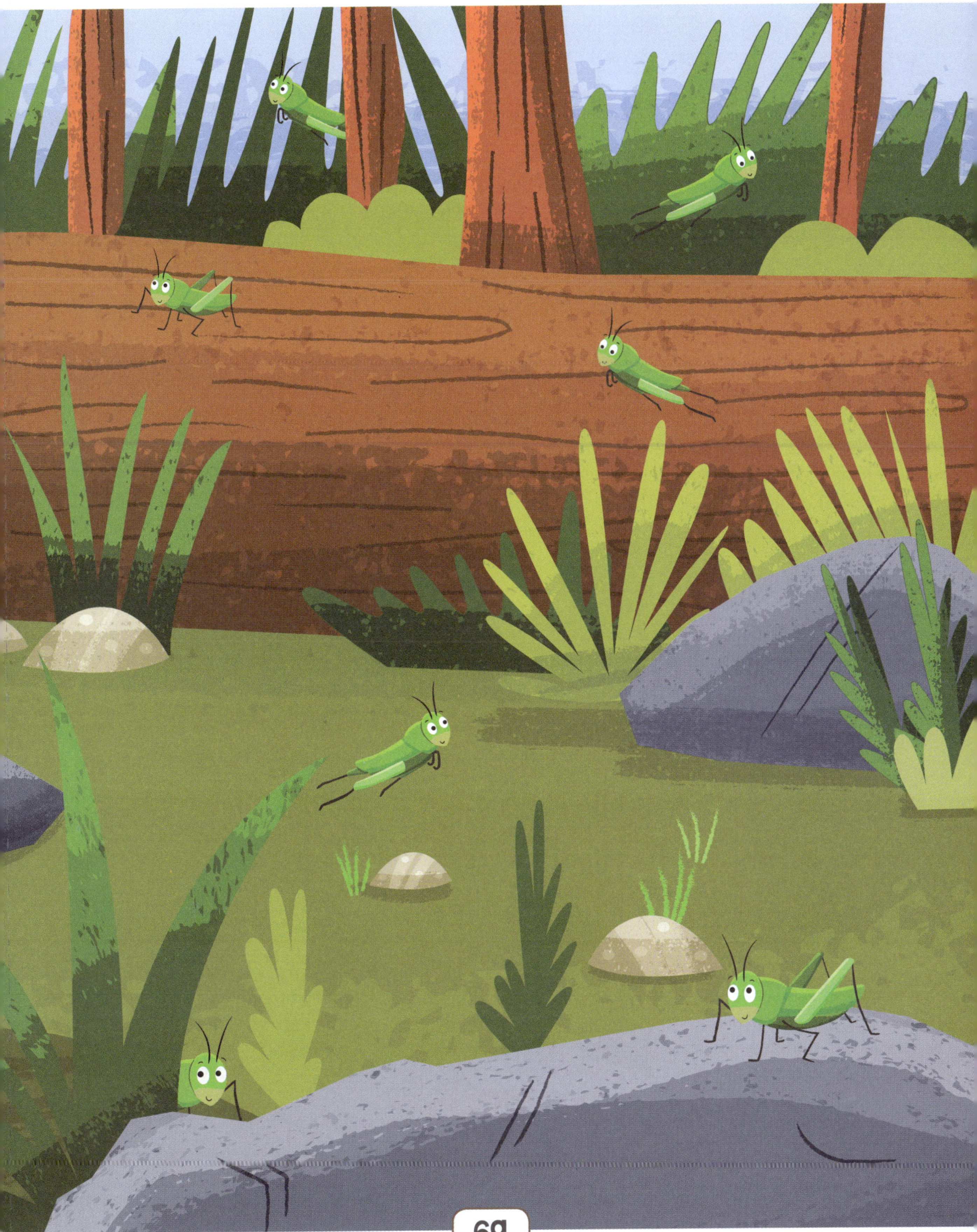

INCHING ALONG

Draw a line from each worm to the leaf beneath it.

70

HUNTING FOR ACORNS

Draw a line from the ➡ to the **End**.

Trace the acorn.

Draw an acorn.

71

ROCK CLIMBER

Draw a line from the ➡ to the **End**.

End

Trace the horn on the sheep.
Color the picture.

72

FOREST CROSSING

Find and circle the hidden pictures.

| centipede | woodpecker | bear print | wolf cub | chipmunk | mushroom |

WHAT'S DIFFERENT?

Find and circle **8** things that are different in **picture A** and **picture B**.

Picture A

74
© School Zone Publishing 06338

Picture B

75

AVIAN CROSSWORD

Use the picture clues to fill in the puzzle.

dove   duck   hawk   heron

Across

1. 
2.

Down

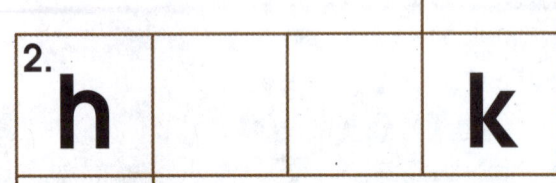

1. 
2.

EAGLE'S NEST

Draw a line from the ➡ to the End.

FUR & FEATHERS

Color the animals with feathers **blue**.
Color the animals with fur **orange**.
Color the animals without fur or feathers **green**.

Are there more animals with fur or feathers? _____

79

HOME TO THE HATCHLINGS

Draw a line from from the blue jay to her hatchlings.

TO VISIT THE QUEEN

Draw a line from the ➡ to the **End**.

Subtract. How many are left?

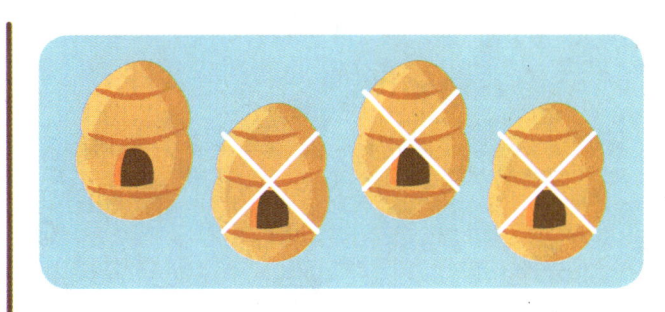

7 - 5 = ___

4 - 3 = ___

81

WHAT'S DIFFERENT?

Find and circle **6** things that are different in **picture A** and **picture B**.

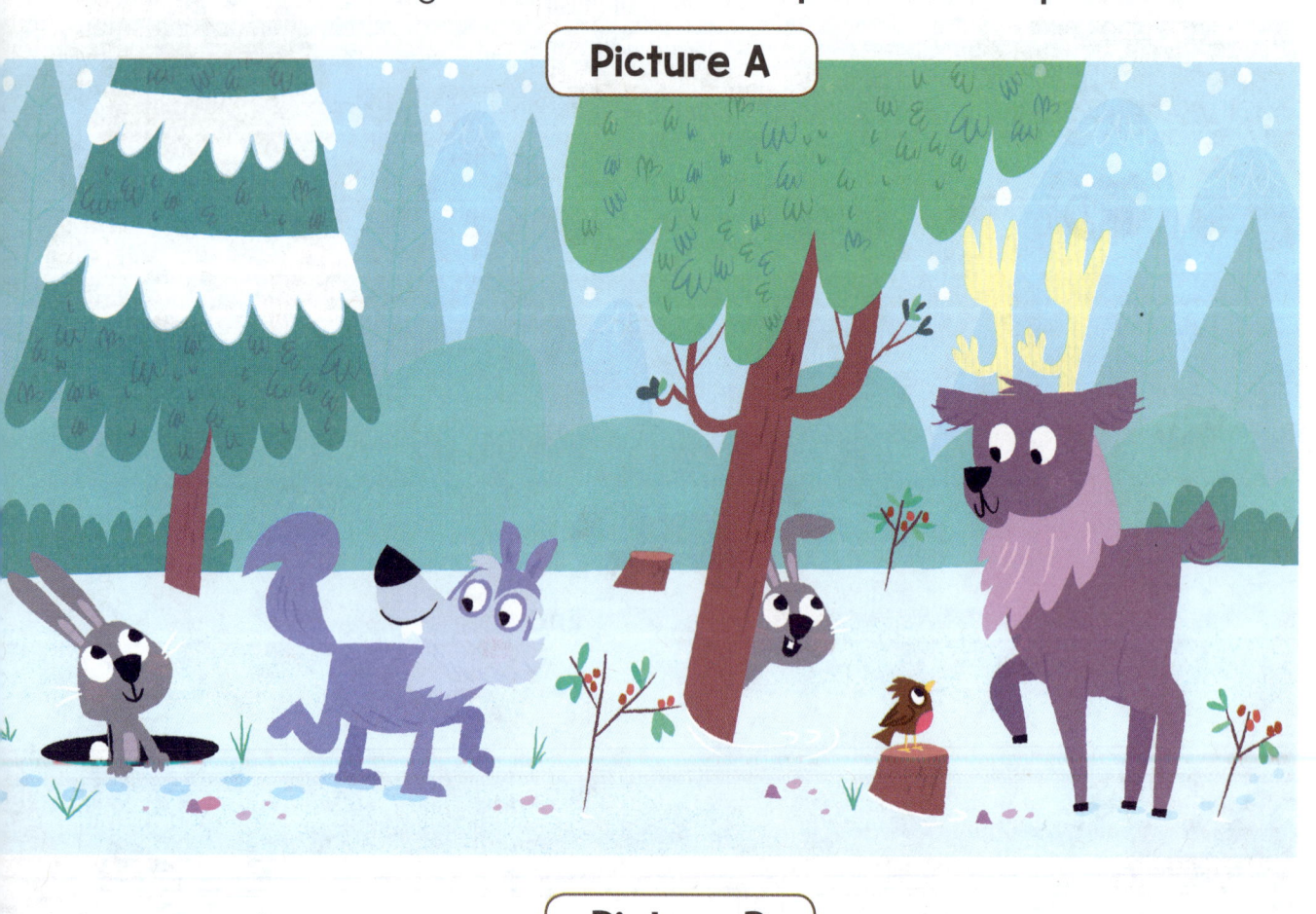

DUNG BEETLE

Connect the dots from 1-20.
Color the picture.

83

MARIPOSA

Connect the dots from 1-20.
Color the picture.

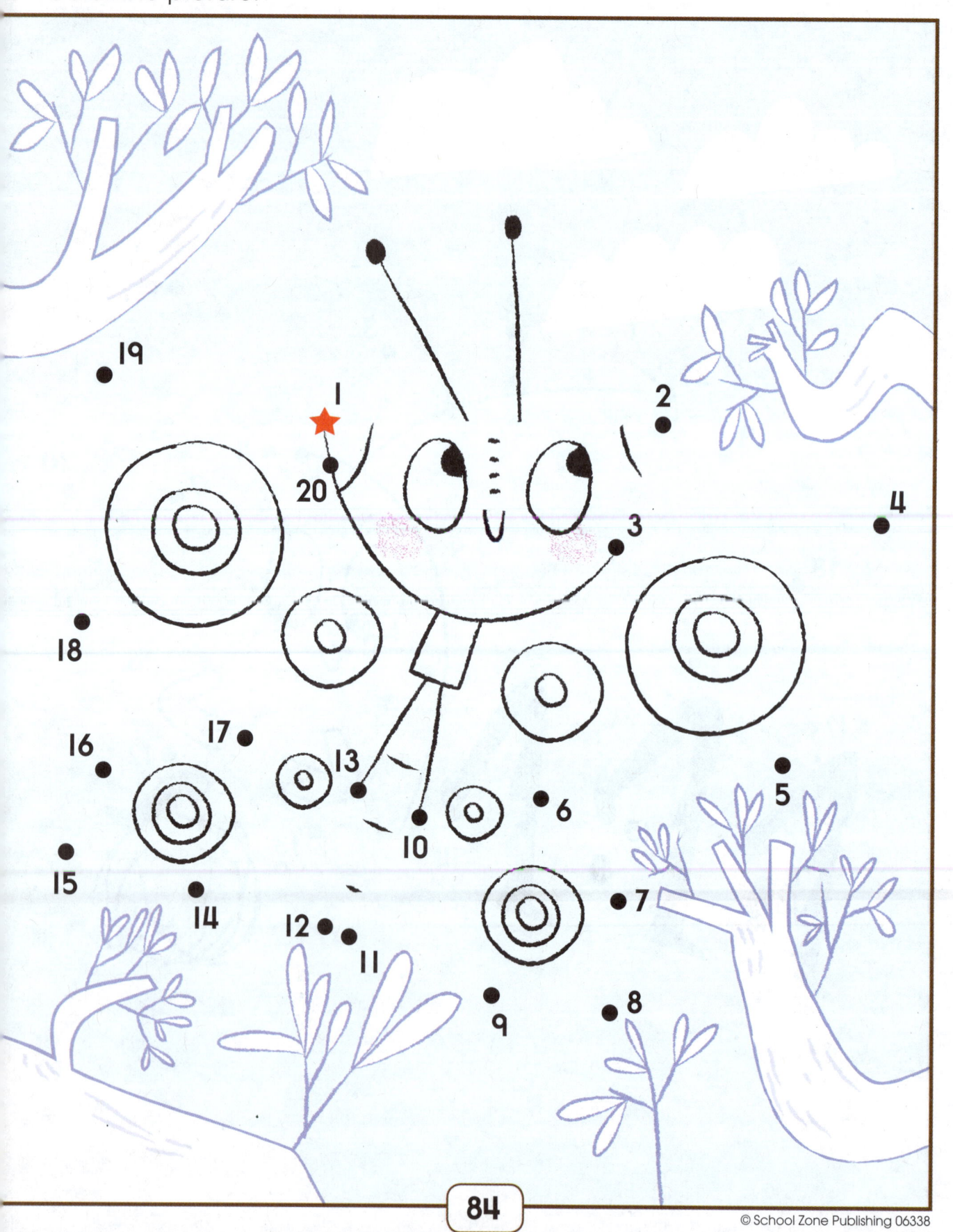

INSECTS & ARACHNIDS

Entomology is the study of insects. **Arachnology** is the study of spiders. Learn some of the differences between insects and arachnids below.

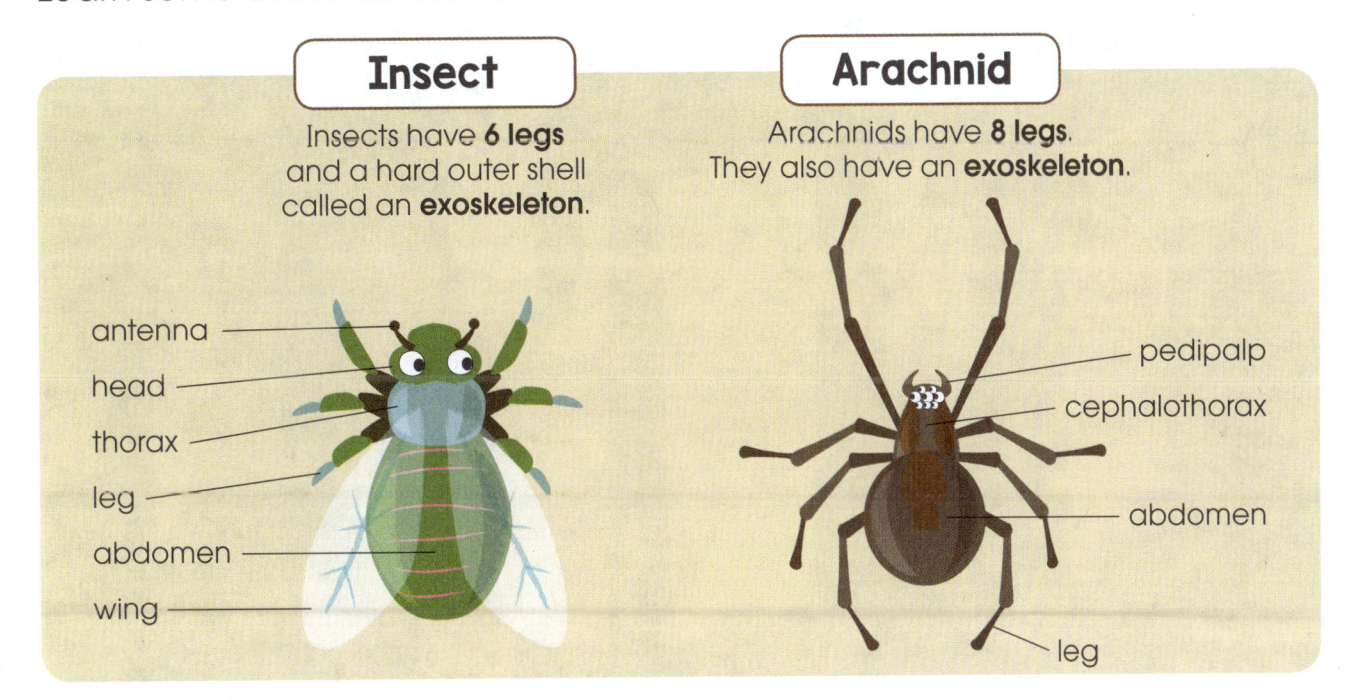

Insect
Insects have **6 legs** and a hard outer shell called an **exoskeleton**.

- antenna
- head
- thorax
- leg
- abdomen
- wing

Arachnid
Arachnids have **8 legs**. They also have an **exoskeleton**.

- pedipalp
- cephalothorax
- abdomen
- leg

Circle the arachnids.
✓ Check the insects.

85
© School Zone Publishing 06338

WHAT'S DIFFERENT?

Find and circle **12** things that are different in **picture A** and **picture B**.

Picture A

Picture B

87

LIFE UNDERGROUND

Draw a line from the ➡ to the **End**.

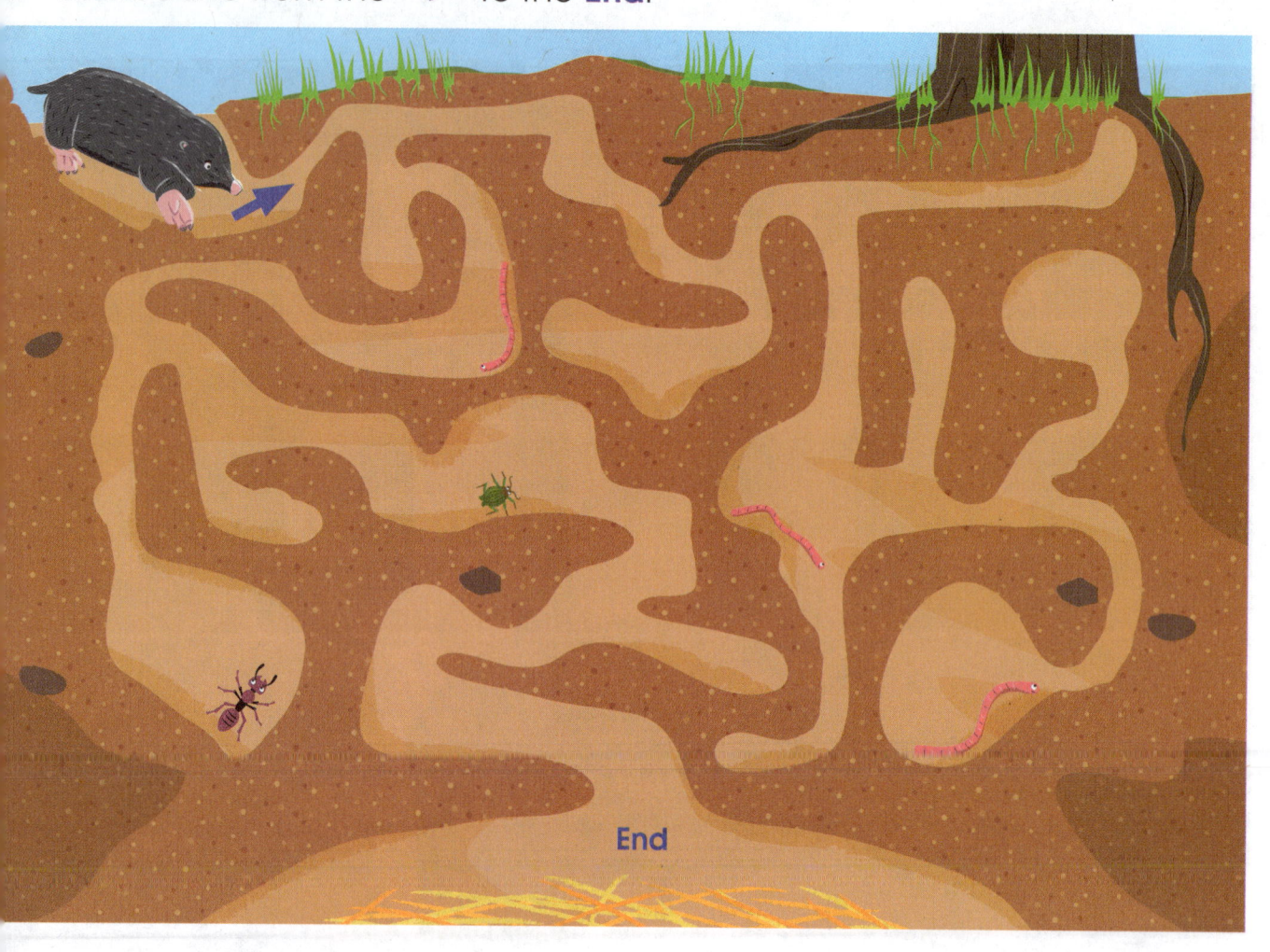

Count the pictures in each group.
Circle the group that has more.

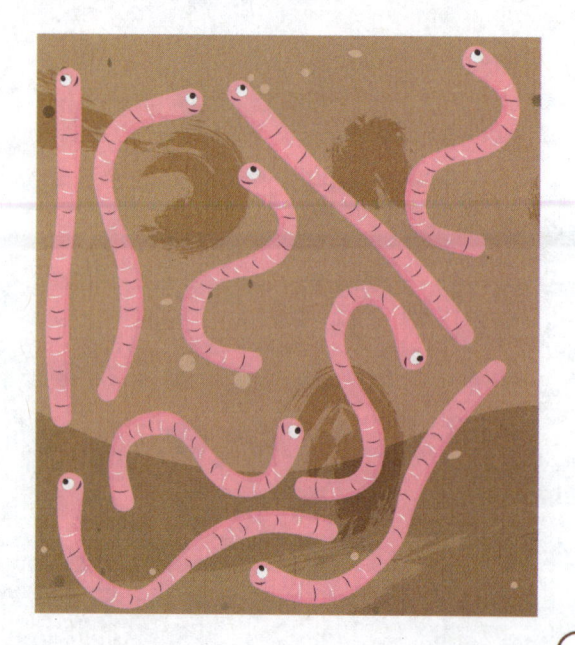

88

FOREST CUTOUTS

Cut out the forest and animal pieces. Fold the paper on the lines to make the pieces stand up. Use the pieces to tell a story using the words **first**, **then**, **next**, and **last**.

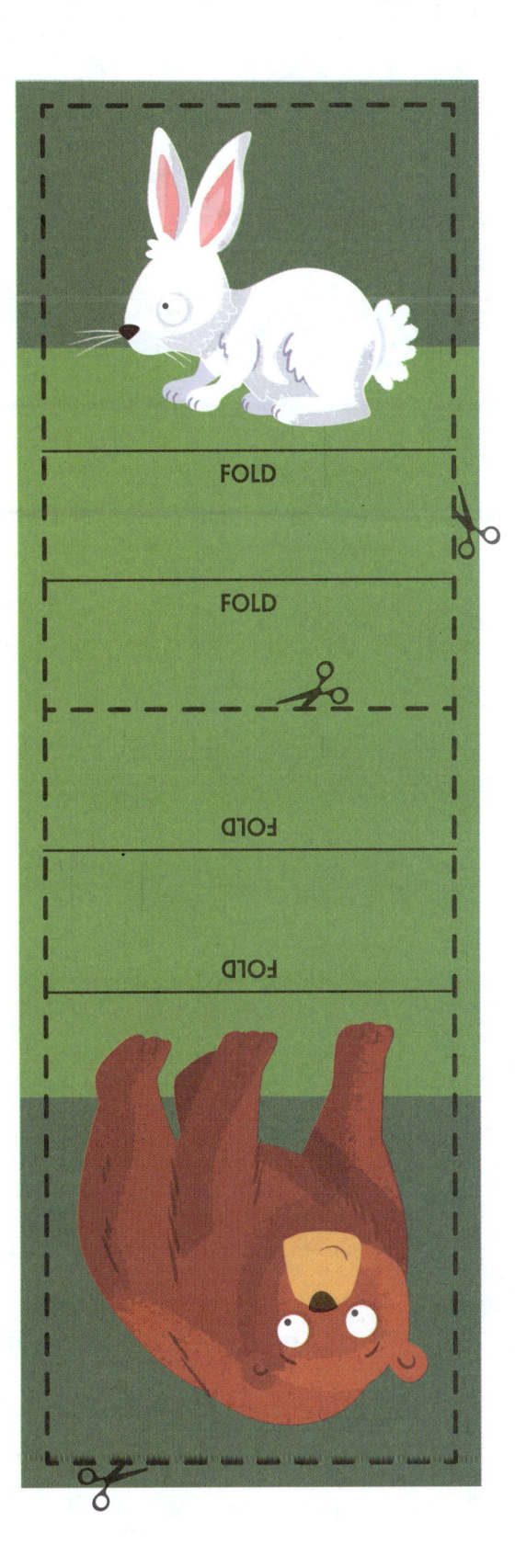

WOODLAND CHIPMUNKS

Find and circle all of the 🐿's in the picture. How many did you find?

BRILLIANT BUTTERFLIES

Color the picture.

- ● = blue
- ● = yellow
- ● = purple
- ● = pink
- ● = orange

92
© School Zone Publishing 06338

THE GREAT HORNED OWL

Cut out the puzzle pieces and mix them up.
Put the puzzle pieces together.

1   2   3   4   5   6

93

94

MASKED MAMMAL

Connect the dots from 1–20.
Color the picture.

95

LEARN TO DRAW

Follow the steps to draw ladybugs and birds.

Step 1:
Draw a **half-circle** for the body.

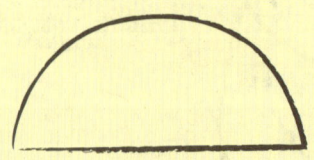

Step 2:
Draw the head.

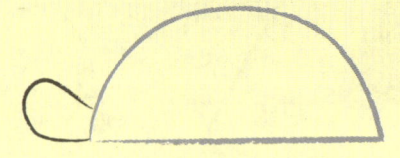

Step 3:
Draw the spots on the back.

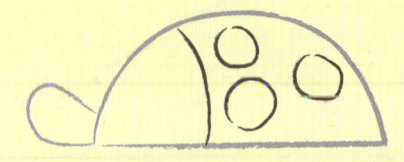

Step 4:
Draw a **dot** for the eye and lines for the antennae and legs.

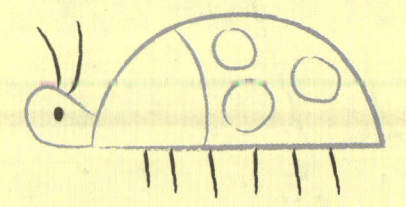

Step 5:
Color in the black areas.

Step 1:
Draw a **circle** for the head.

Step 2:
Draw an **oval** for the body and a **triangle** for the beak.

Step 3:
Draw the wings and tail.

Step 4:
Draw **dots** for the eyes and lines for the feathers and legs.

97

WHAT'S DIFFERENT?

Find and circle **12** things that are different in **picture A** and **picture B**.

Picture A

Picture B

LEARN TO DRAW

Step 1:
Draw a **circle** for the head.

Step 2:
Draw a **half-oval** for the beak and the body.

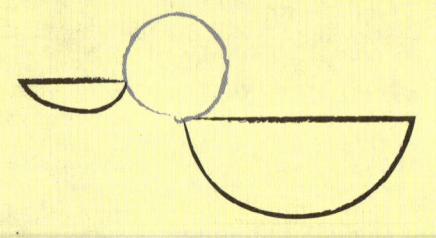

Step 3:
Draw a line for the wing and tail feathers.

Step 4:
Draw a **dot** for the eye and lines for the legs.

Follow the steps to draw ducks and dragonflies.

© School Zone Publishing 06338

Step 1:
Draw a **circle** for the head.

Step 2:
Draw a **circle** and a long **oval** for the body.

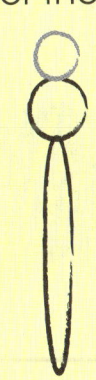

Step 3:
Draw the wings.

Step 4:
Draw **dots** for the eyes and lines on the body.

FOREST FAUNA

Find the pictures below, and then check the box next to the picture.

☐ 1 bear

☐ 1 deer

☐ 2 foxes

☐ 3 cardinals

☐ 3 rabbits

☐ 1 badger

102

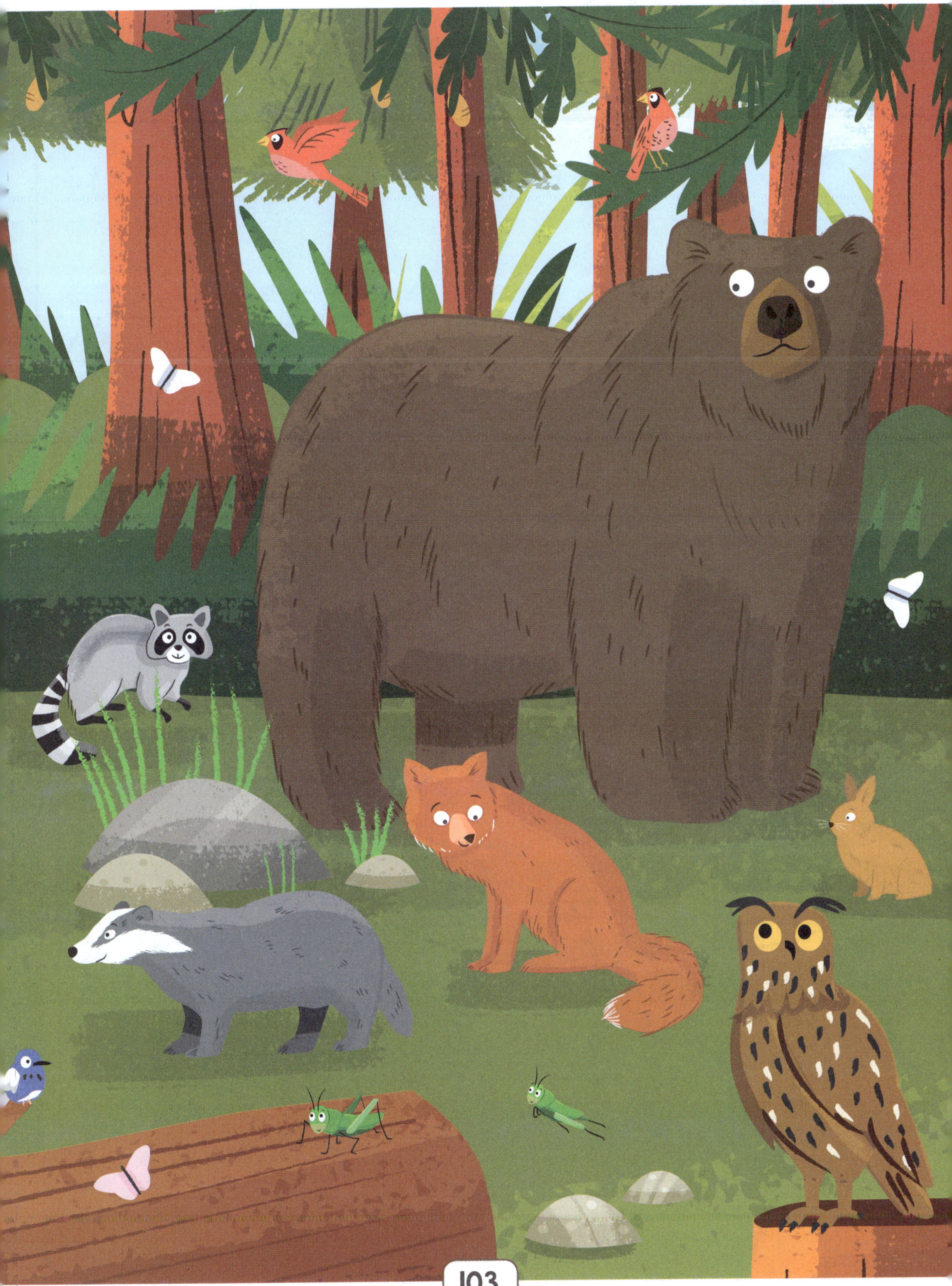

SLIMING ALONG

Connect the dots from 1–25.
Color the picture.

104

CHIPMUNK!

Find and circle the picture that matches this one:

IT'S ALIVE!

Circle the things that are alive.

BEAR CUB RESCUE

Draw a line from the ➡ to the **End**.

WHAT'S DIFFERENT?

Find and circle **7** things that are different in **picture A** and **picture B**.

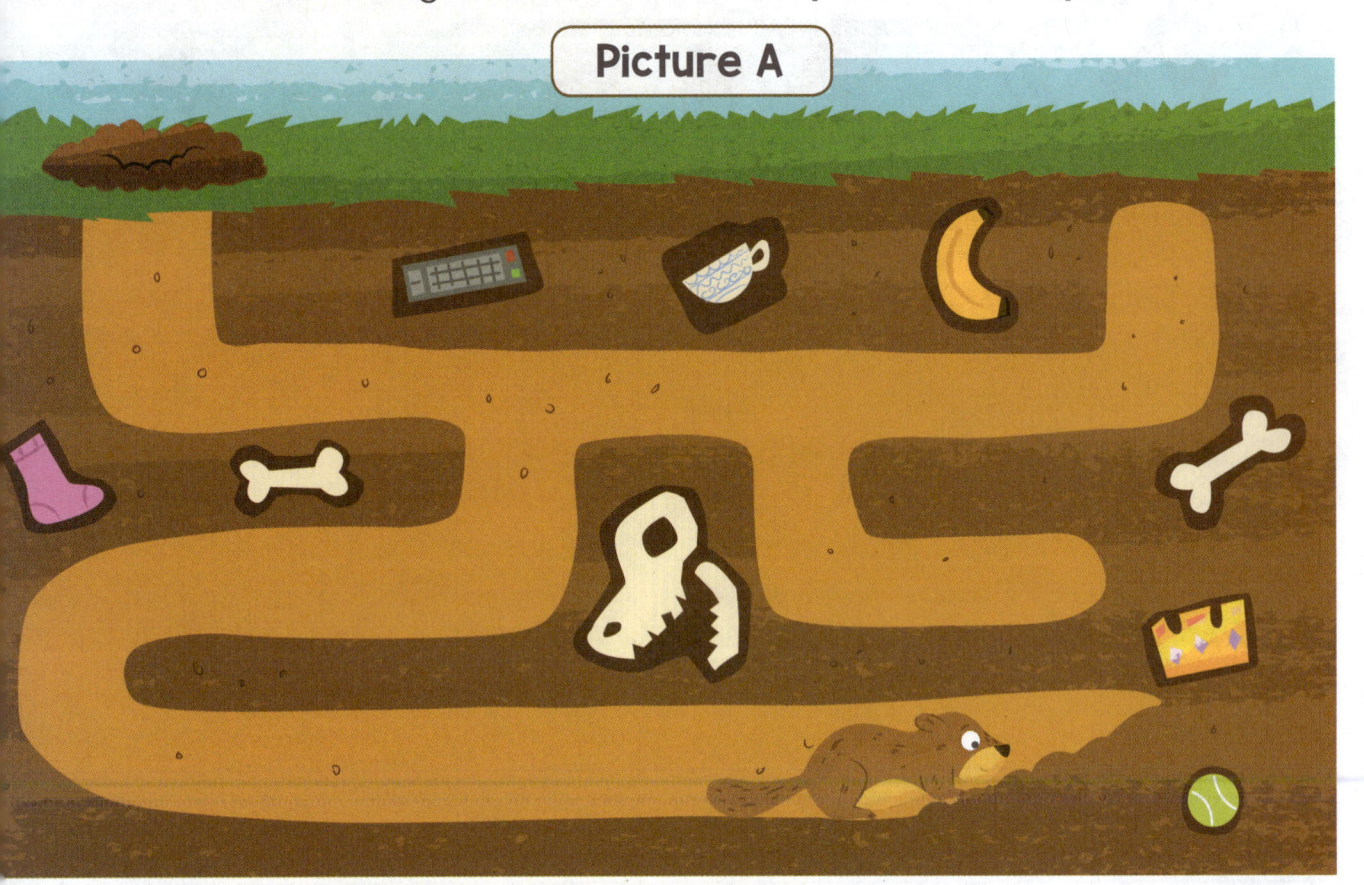

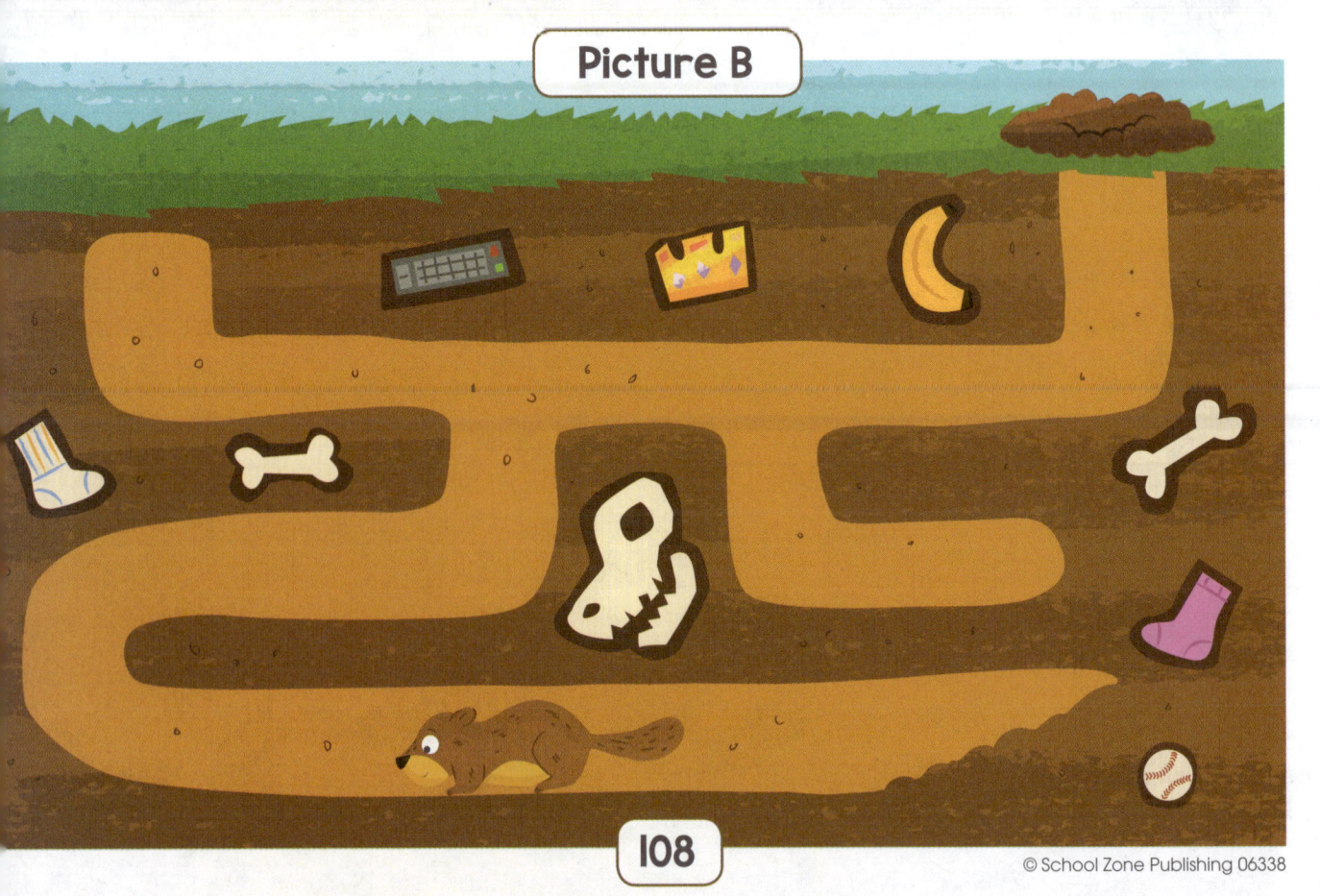

Picture A

Picture B

108

© School Zone Publishing 06338

MR. GOPHER

Color the picture.

● = tan   ● = orange   ● = brown
● = green   ● = blue   ● = pink

RACE THROUGH THE BURROW

Draw a line from each ➡ to each **End**.

CREEPY CRAWLIES

Count the purple bugs. How many did you find?
Count the red bugs. How many did you find?

OUT OF HIBERNATION

Connect the dots from 1-25.
Color the picture.

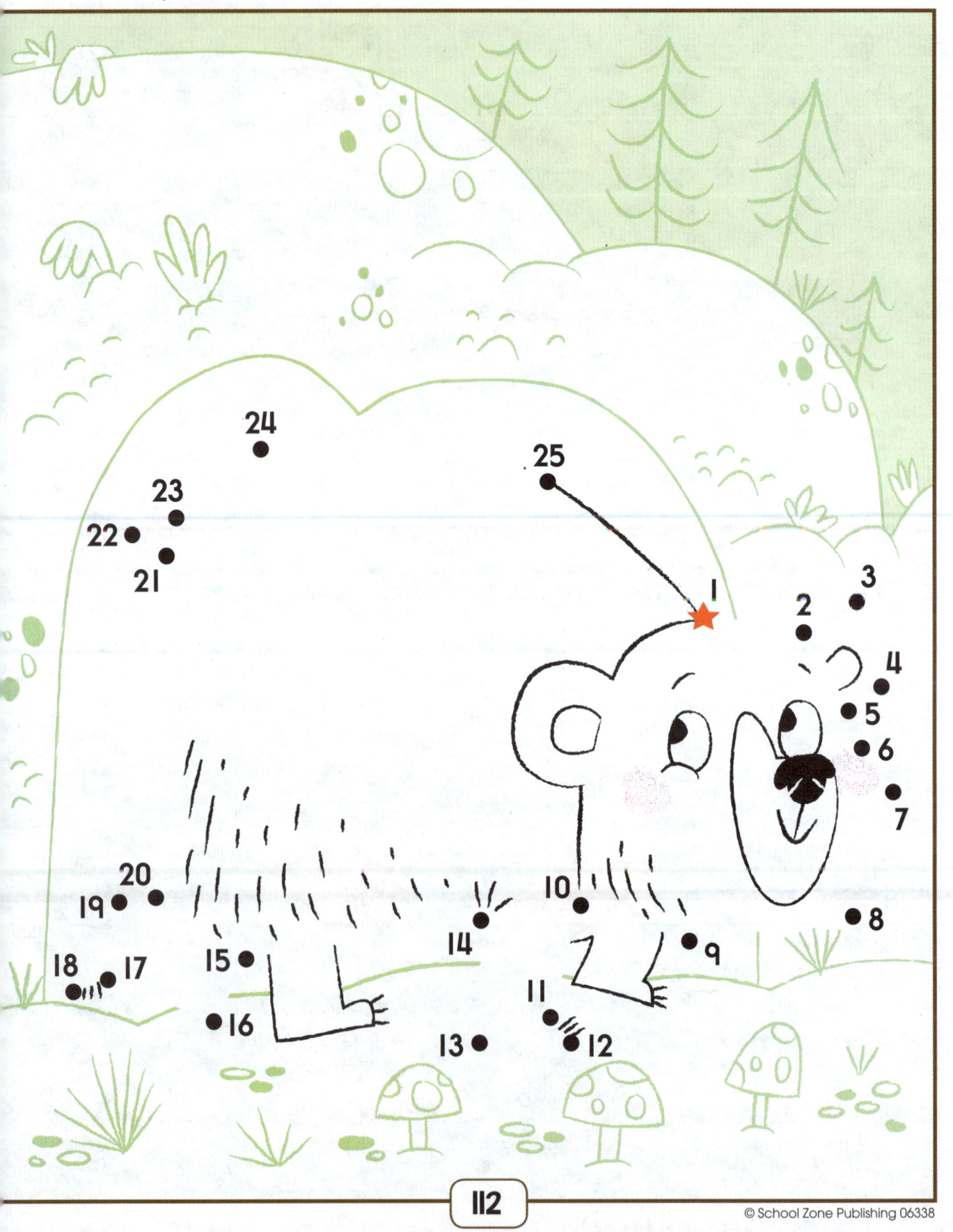

PEAFOWL PLUMAGE

Cut out the puzzle pieces and mix them up.
Put the puzzle pieces together.

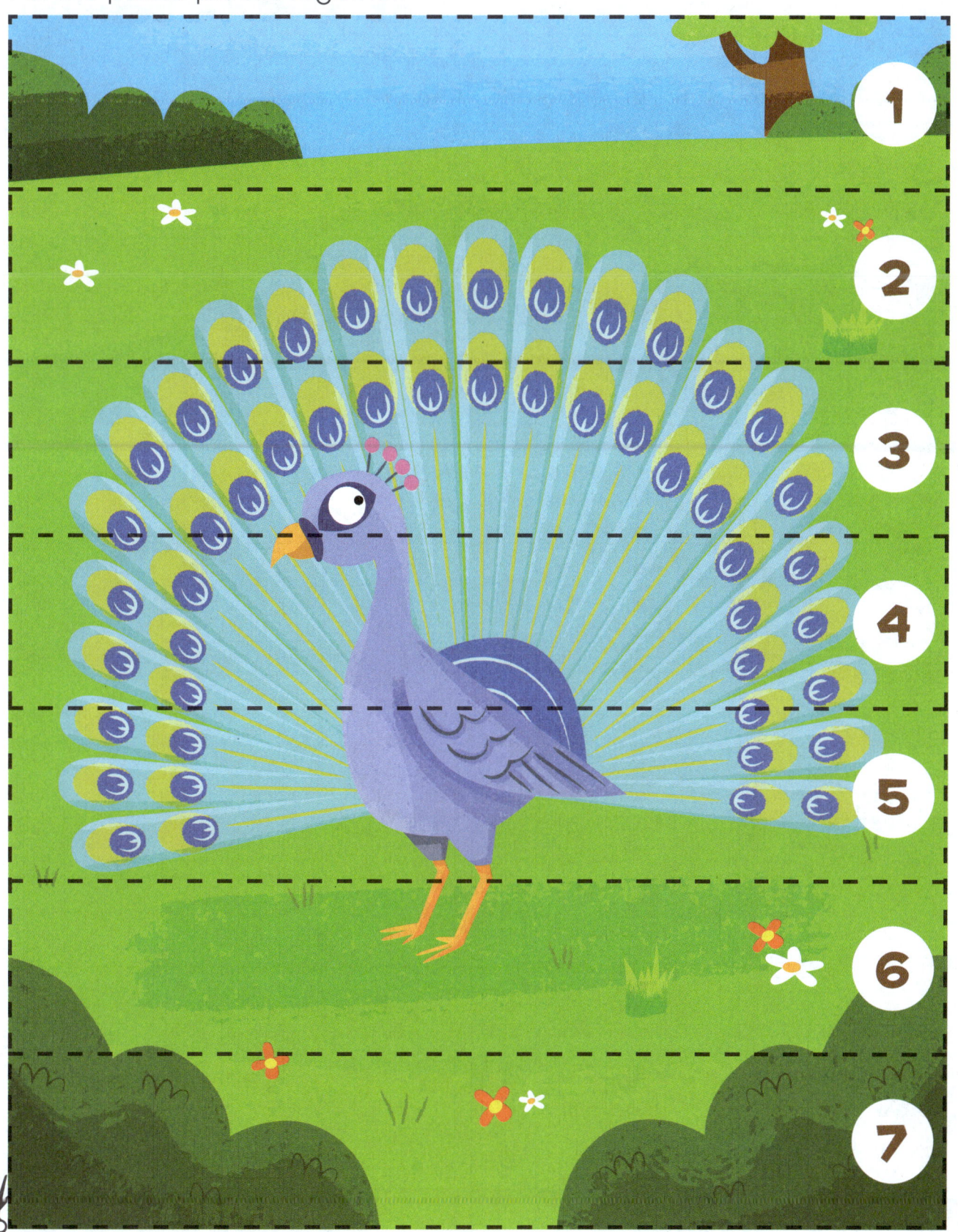

113

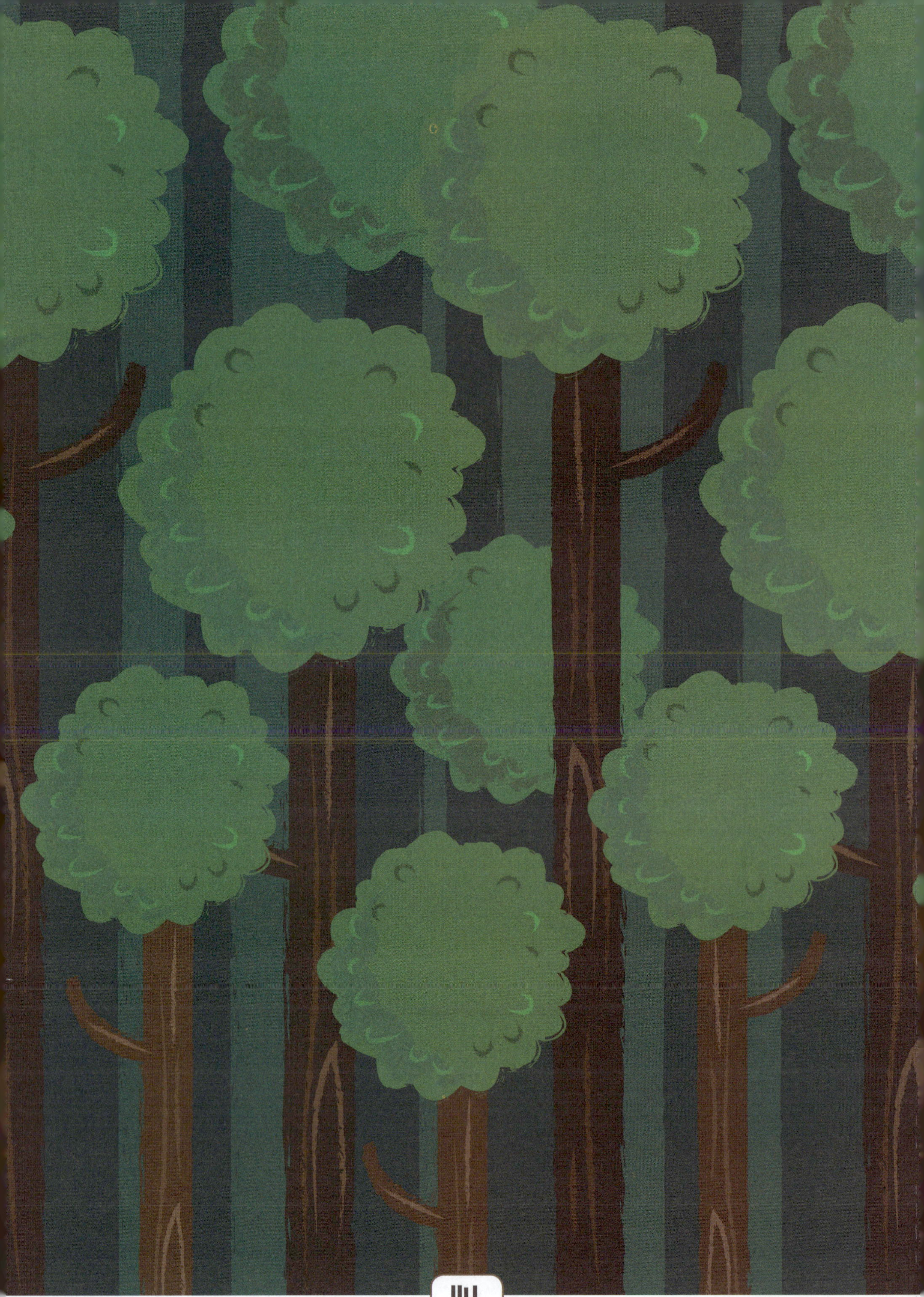

ALAULA KOALA'S CLIMB

Connect the dots from 1–25.
Color the picture.

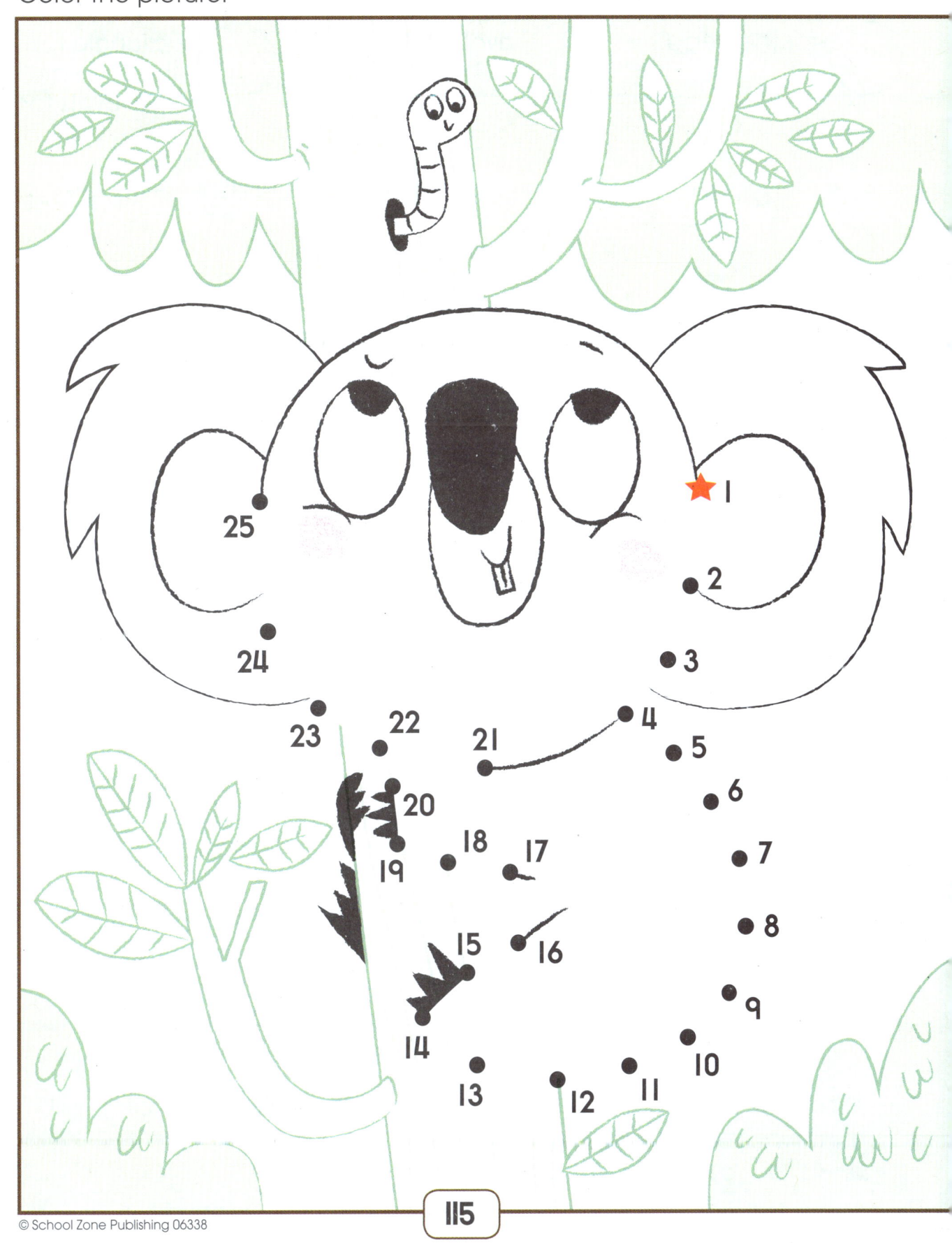

115

LEARN TO DRAW

Step 1: Draw a **circle** for the head.

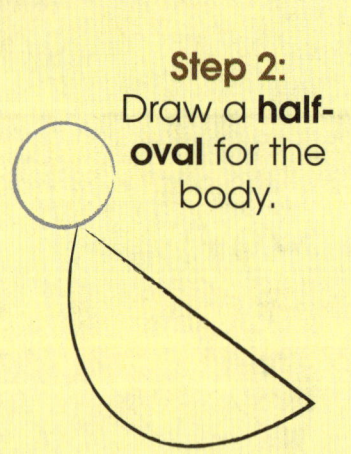

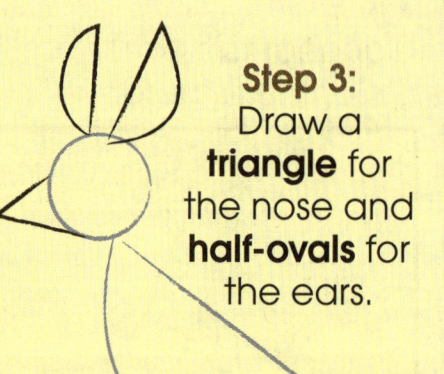

Step 2: Draw a **half-oval** for the body.

Step 3: Draw a **triangle** for the nose and **half-ovals** for the ears.

Follow the steps to draw kangaroos.

Step 4:
Draw lines for the arms, legs, and tail.

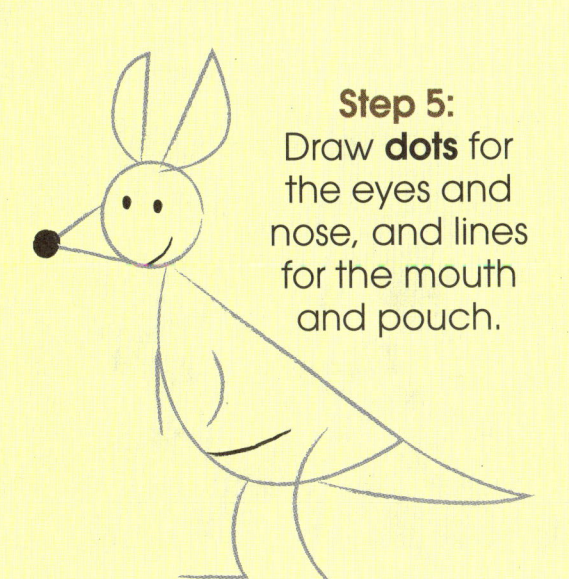

Step 5:
Draw **dots** for the eyes and nose, and lines for the mouth and pouch.

THE WOMBATS GO HOME

Draw a line from the ➡ to the **End**.

End

A MOB OF ROOS

Find and circle the picture that matches this one:

121

RABBIT VISITS THE GARDEN

Look at the word list.
Circle the words in the puzzle.

LADYBUG   ANT   MOLE   SNAKE   RABBIT   GRASSHOPPER   BEE

```
G U E U X W P E Y F H
R Y L A D Y B U G K U
A W Z M J L G Z W Z O
S M T P R N J Z N E H
S J J M G B C R B S L
H K N T Y E Z A U Z Z
O X G G A E S R K H M
P F W G R A B B I T R
P B X A N T Q R K G O
E A Z U S N A K E A P
R V O Z X M O L E Q J
```

122

AUSTRALIAN FOREST CUTOUTS

Cut out the forest and animal pieces. Fold the paper on the lines to make the pieces stand up. Use the pieces to tell a story using the words **first**, **then**, **next**, and **last**.

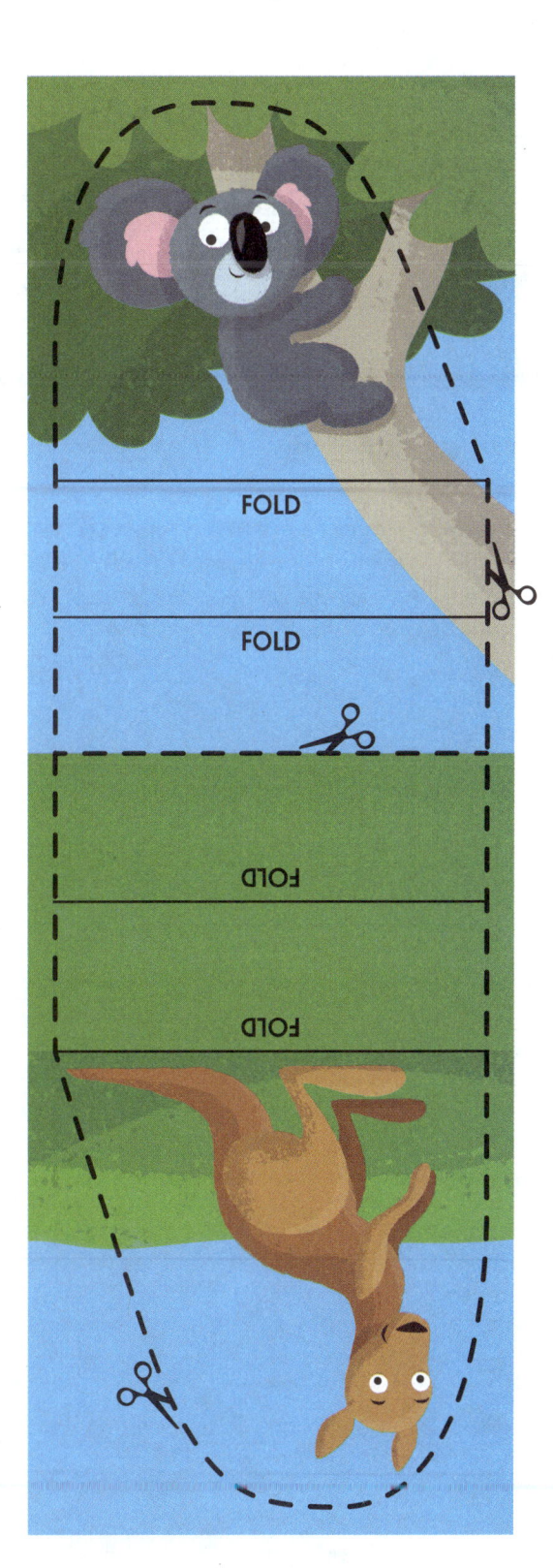

FOLD

FOLD

FOLD

FOLD

FOLD

123

© School Zone Publishing 06338

BUTTERFLIES

Find and circle the picture that matches this one:

125

LEARN TO DRAW

Step 1:
Draw an **oval** for the body.

Step 2:
Draw lines for the wings and stinger.

Step 3:
Draw lines for the stripes.

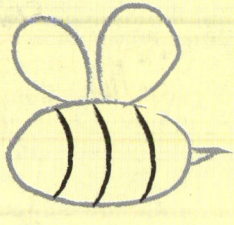

Step 4:
Draw a **dot** for the eye and lines for the mouth and legs.

Step 5:
Color in the black areas.

Follow the steps to draw bees.

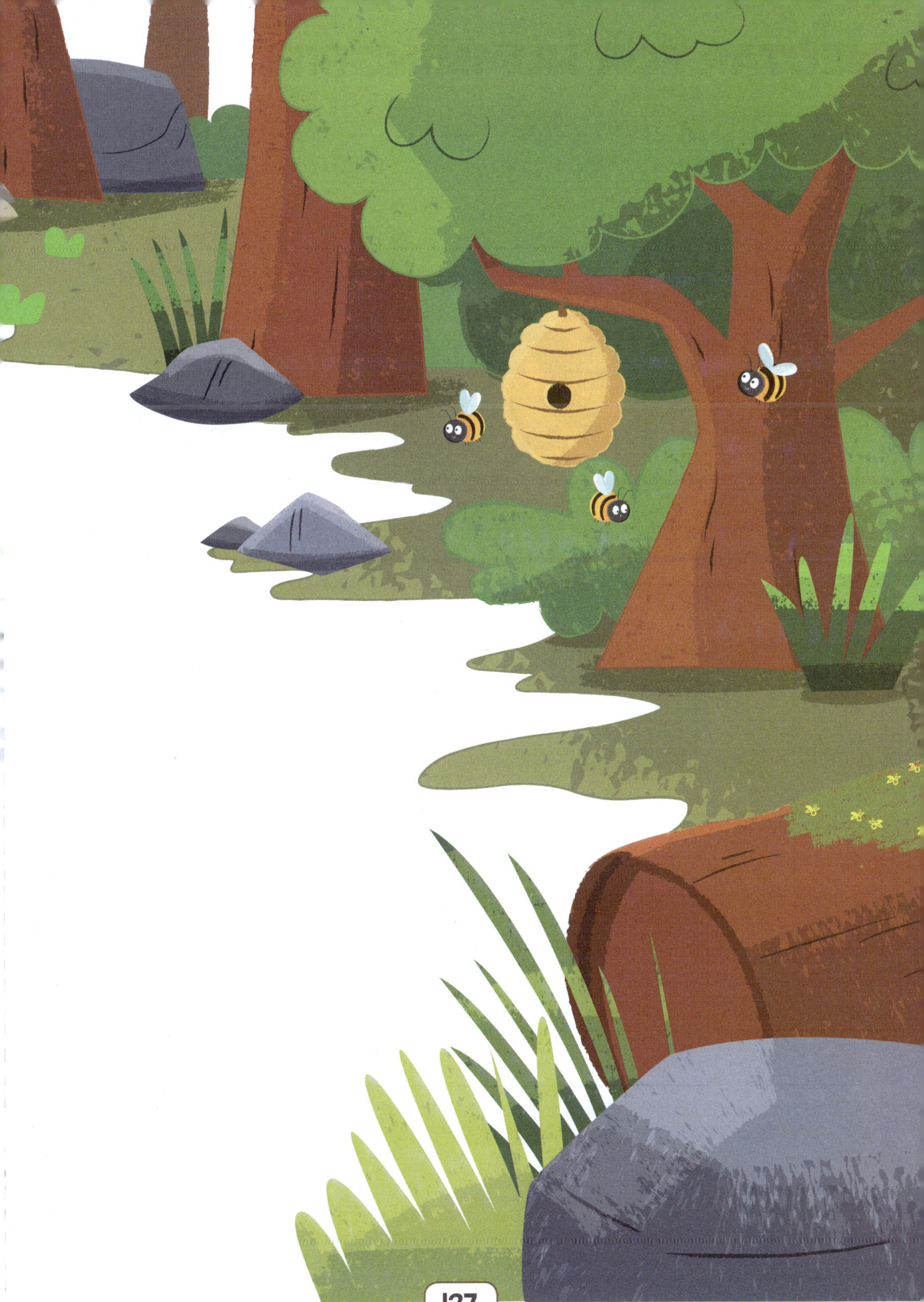

NECTAR FOR HUMMINGBIRDS

Draw a line from each hummingbird to the flowers.

128

BUGS, BUGS, BUGS!

Find and circle all of the bugs that are *orange*. How many did you find?

WHAT'S DIFFERENT?

Find and circle **12** things that are different in **picture A** and **picture B**.

Picture A

Picture B

LEARN TO DRAW

Step 1:
Draw a **circle** for the shell.

Step 2:
Draw a line on the bottom of the shell.

Step 3:
Draw a line for the body.

Follow the steps to draw snails.

Step 4:
Draw lines for the eye tentacles and the mouth.

Step 5:
Draw **dots** for the eyes and a **spiral** on the shell.

RED FOX

Color the picture.

- 🔴 = red
- 🟡 = yellow
- 🟢 = dark green
- 🟤 = brown
- 🟢 = green
- ⚫ = black

134

BUTTERFLY GARDEN CUTOUTS

Cut out the garden and butterfly pieces. Fold the paper on the lines to make the pieces stand up. Use the pieces to tell a story using the words **first**, **then**, **next**, and **last**.

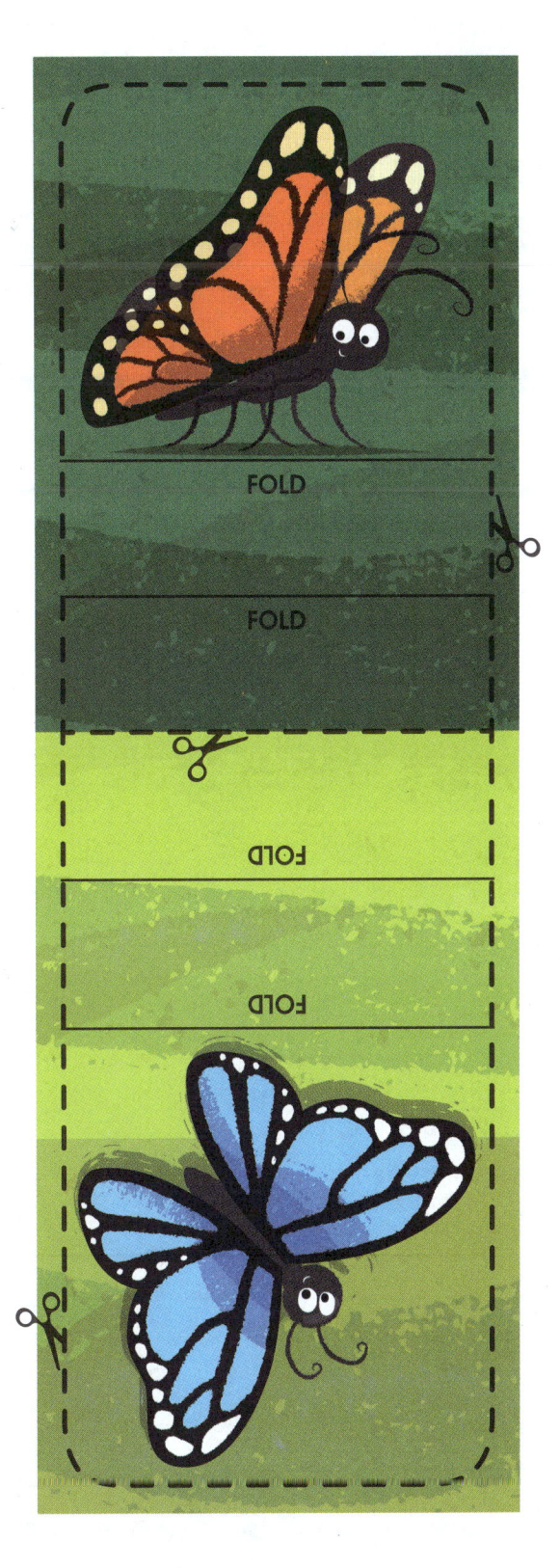

135

THE FASTEST CAT

Connect the dots from 1–25.
Color the picture.

137

WHAT'S DIFFERENT?

Find and circle **12** things that are different in **picture A** and **picture B**.

Picture A

138
© School Zone Publishing 06338

Picture B

KING OF THE BEASTS

Trace the lines to finish drawing the lion.
Color the lion.

SAVANNA FUN

Cut out the puzzle pieces and mix them up.
Put the puzzle pieces together.

1 2 3 4 5 6 7

141

BE THE LION!

Cut out the lion mask. Cut along the straight lines to make the lion's mane. If you need to, ask for a grown-up's help.

You can also tape a popsicle stick or a straight drinking straw to the back of the mask to make it easier to hold the mask up to your face.

Two more masks can be found in this book:

Zebra Mask (page 155)

Alligator Mask (page 273)

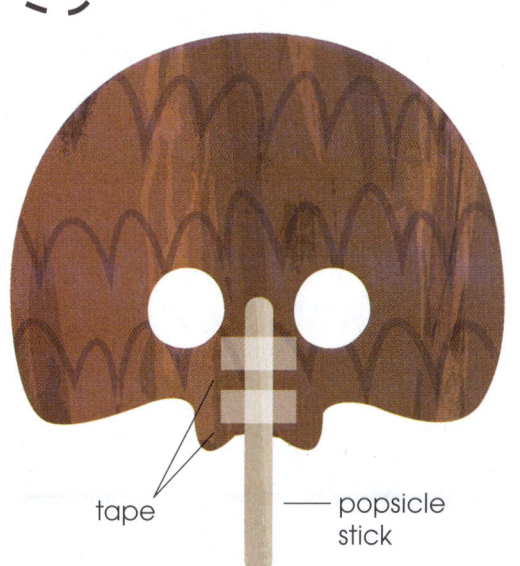

back of mask

tape

popsicle stick

143

© School Zone Publishing 06338

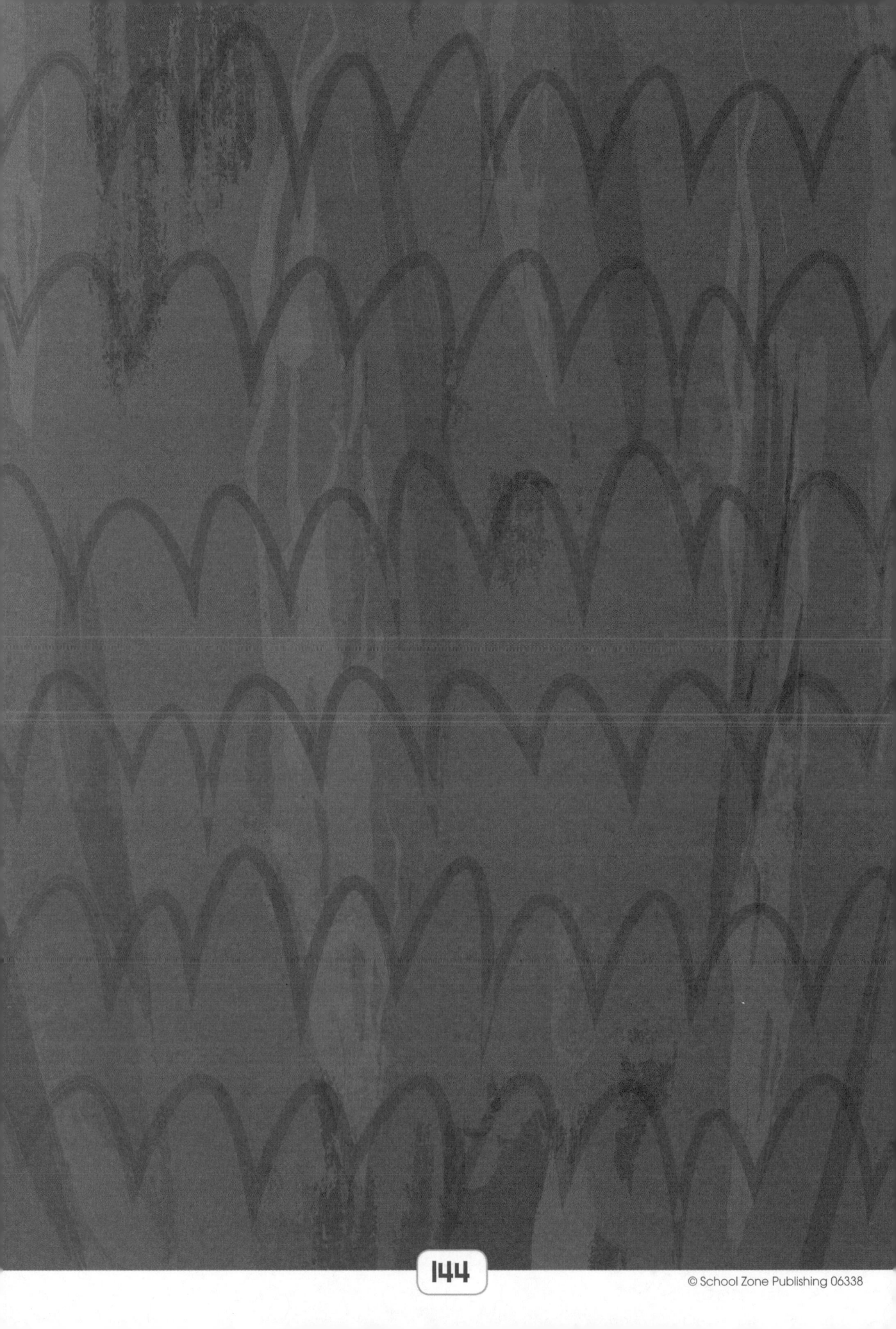

ELEPHANT BATHTIME

Connect the dots from 1–25.
Color the picture.

145

SAVANNA SILLINESS

Find and circle all of the silly things in the scene. How many did you find?

A GIRAFFE AND HER CALF

Cut out the puzzle pieces and mix them up.
Put the puzzle pieces together.

147

WHAT'S DIFFERENT?

Find and circle **6** things that are different in **picture A** and **picture B**.

Picture A

Picture B

149

LEARN TO DRAW

Follow the steps to draw flamingos.

Step 1:
Draw a **circle** for the head and a curved line for the neck.

Step 2:
Draw a **half-oval** for the body and beak.

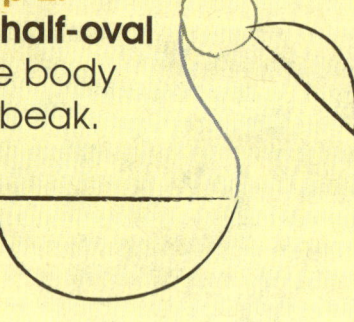

Step 3:
Draw the wing, the tail feathers, and a line on the beak.

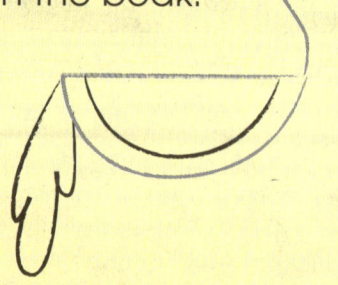

Step 4:
Draw a **dot** for the eye and lines for the mouth and legs.

150

© School Zone Publishing 06338

151

ZEBRA STRIPES

Trace the zebra's stripes. Color the picture.

GRACEFUL GAZELLE

Connect the dots from 1–25.
Color the picture.

153

HORNBILL WILLIAM

Trace the drawing of the hornbill.
Color the picture to match this one:

154

BE THE ZEBRA!

Cut out the zebra mask. If you need to, ask for a grown-up's help.

You can also tape a popsicle stick or a straight drinking straw to the back of the mask to make it easier to hold the mask up to your face.

Two more masks can be found in this book:

Lion Mask (page 143)

Alligator Mask (page 273)

back of mask

tape

popsicle stick

155

© School Zone Publishing 06338

WHAT'S DIFFERENT?

Find and circle **6** things that are different in **picture A** and **picture B**.

Picture A

Picture B

157

RONNY RHINO'S JAUNT

Draw a line from the ➡ to the **End**.

KOOKY SAFARI

Find and circle all of the silly things in the scene.

PIN THE TAILS

Draw a line from the animal to the matching tail.

160

AS TALL AS A TREE

Connect the dots from 1-25.
Color the picture.

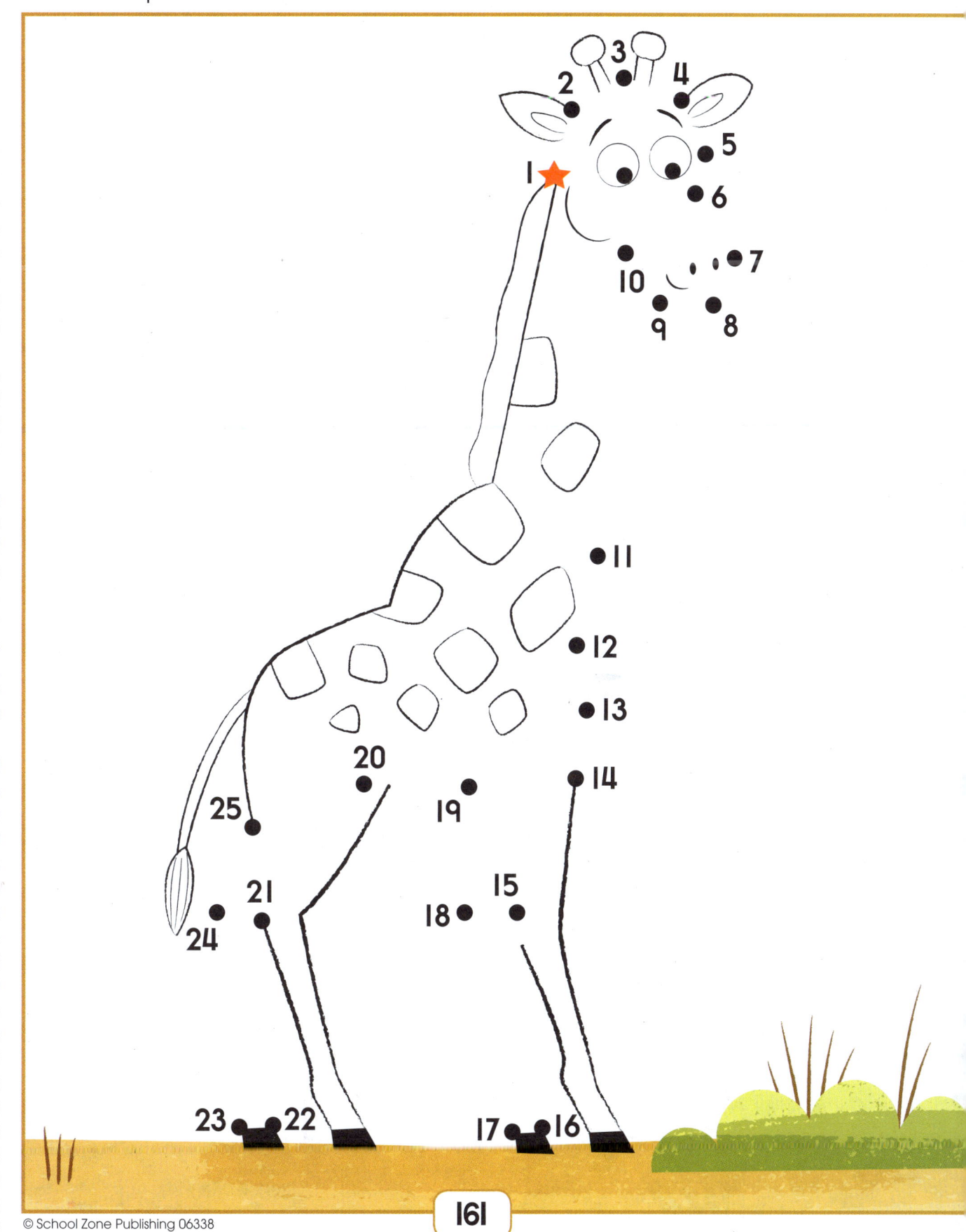

161

LEARN TO DRAW

Step 1: Draw a **circle** for the head.

Step 2: Draw an **oval** for the snout.

Step 3: Draw a big **oval** for the body.

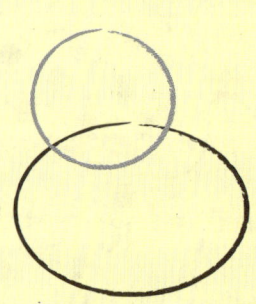

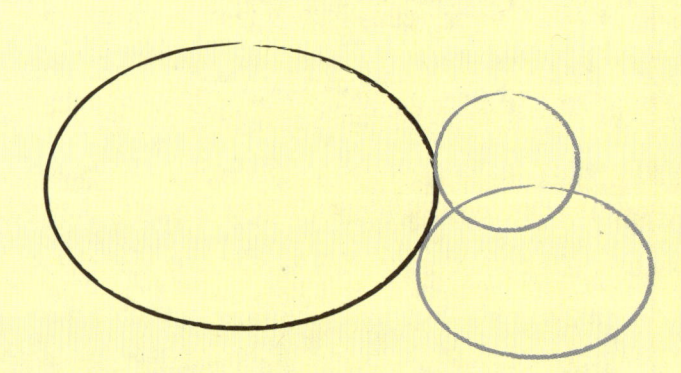

Follow the steps to draw hippos.

Step 4:
Draw the lines for the legs and ears.

Step 5:
Draw **dots** for the eyes, **circles** for the nose, and lines for the teeth, toenails, and tail.

HIPPOPOTAMUS

Connect the dots from 1–25.
Color the picture.

164

THE WATERING HOLE

Cut out the puzzle pieces and mix them up.
Put the puzzle pieces together.

3 4 5 6 7 8

165

ELEPHANT ANTICS

Color the picture.

- ● = pink
- ● = blue
- ● = orange
- ● = yellow
- ● = purple

167

OUT OF PLACE

Circle the animal that does not belong.

WHAT'S DIFFERENT?

Find and circle **7** things that are different in **picture A** and **picture B**.

Picture A

Picture B

169
© School Zone Publishing 06338

ORCA AND CALF

Connect the dots from 1–25.
Color the picture.

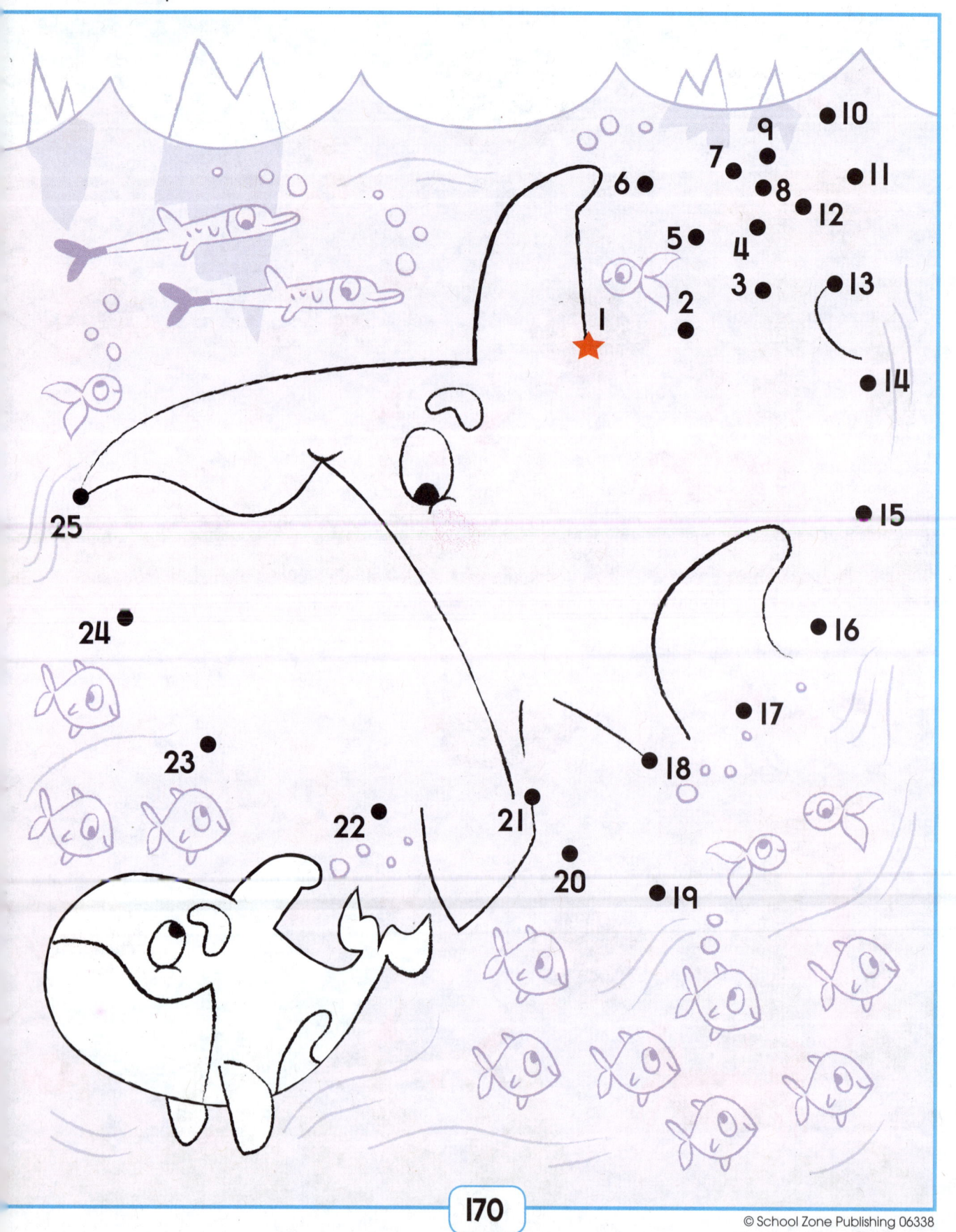

170

EQUINE OF THE SEA

Color the picture.

● = green   ● = orange   ● = pink
● = blue   ● = yellow   ● = dark blue

171

SO MANY FISH

Find and circle the fish that are exactly the same as these:

173

CRUSTACEAN ELATION

Trace the lines to finish drawing the crab.
Color the crab.

174

HELLO, OCTOPUS!

Color the picture.

- = teal
- = purple
- = pink
- = green

175

WHAT'S DIFFERENT?

Find and circle **6** things that are different in **picture A** and **picture B**.

Picture A

176

Picture B

CLOWNFISH SWIMS ALONG

Draw a line from the ➡ to the **End**.

Color the clownfish to match the picture.

178

OCEAN CUTOUTS

Cut out the ocean animal pieces. Fold the paper on the lines to make the pieces stand up. Use the pieces to tell a story using the words **first**, **then**, **next**, and **last**.

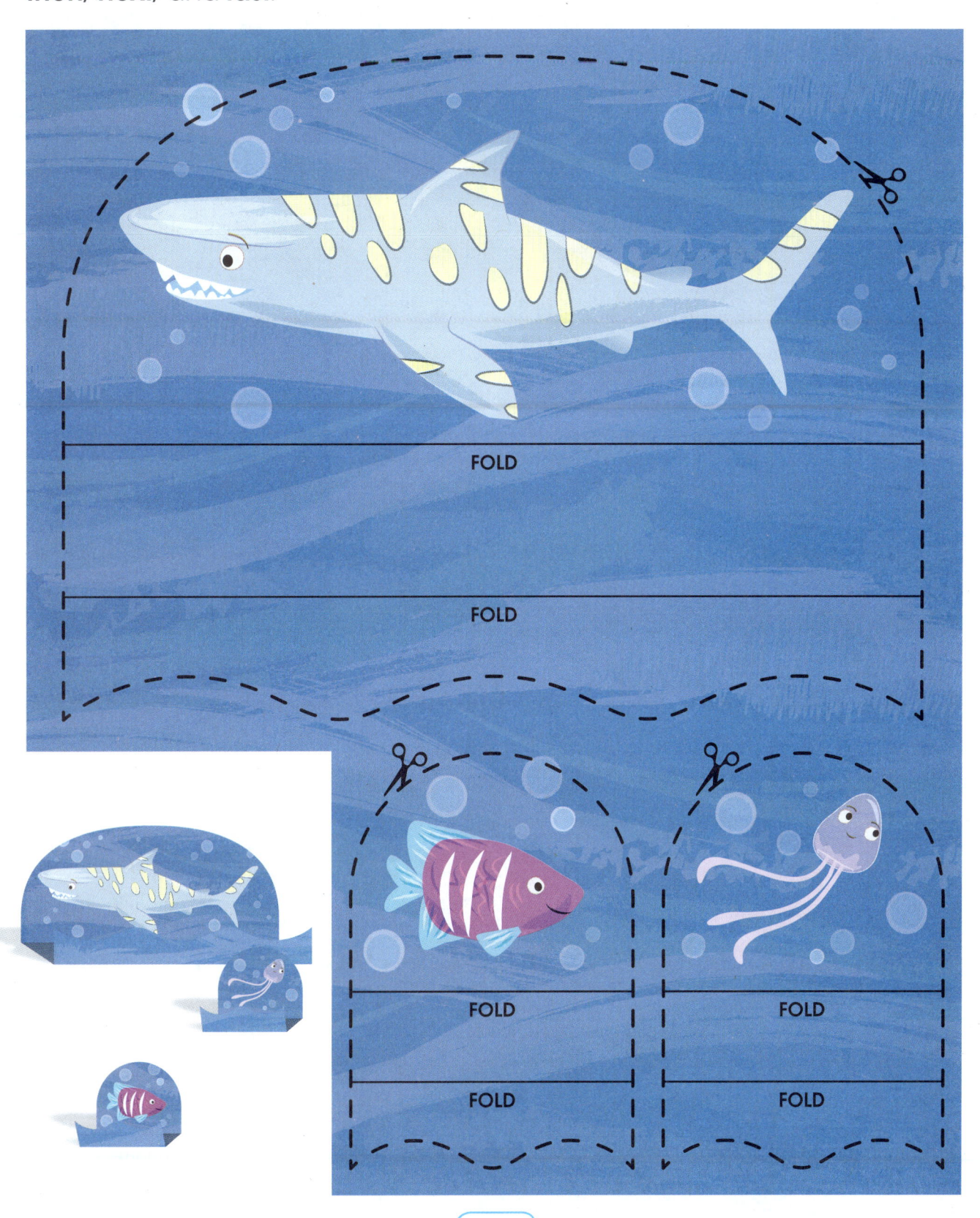

FOLD

FOLD

FOLD

FOLD

FOLD

FOLD

179

STARFISH & SEASHELLS

Color the picture.

- ● = tan
- ● = red
- ● = dark blue
- ● = pink
- ● = blue
- ● = yellow

181

SHARK SIMILARITIES

Find and circle the two sharks that are exactly the same.

182

REEF LIFE

Color the picture.

- ● = gray
- ● = pink
- ● = yellow
- ● = purple
- ● = red
- ● = orange

UNDERSEA SHADOWS

Draw a line from each animal to its shadow.

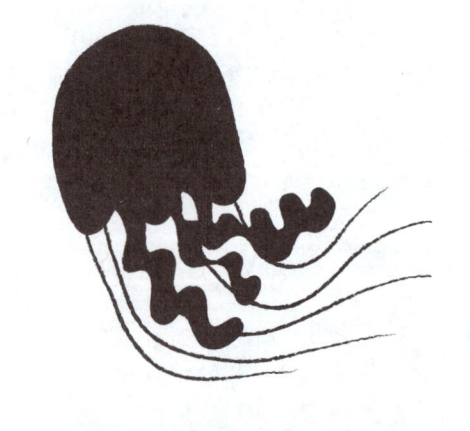

DAY AT THE BEACH

Cut out the puzzle pieces and mix them up.
Put the puzzle pieces together.

185

QUEST TO THE OCEAN

Draw a line from the ➡ to the End.

Color the turtles to complete the patterns.

187

LEARN TO DRAW

Step 1:
Draw a **half-oval** for the body.

Step 2:
Draw lines for the tail.

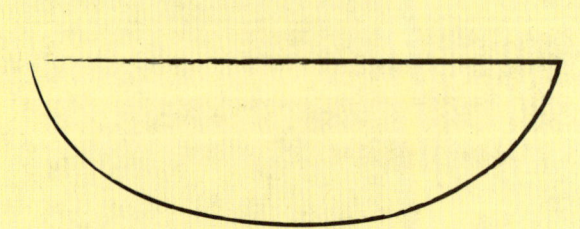

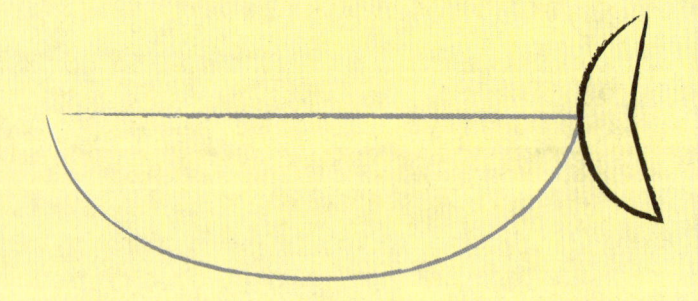

Follow the steps to draw sharks.

Step 3:
Draw a **triangle** for the top fin and a **half-circle** for the side fin.

Step 4:
Draw a **dot** for the eye and lines for the gills and mouth.

CRABBY COPIES

Find and circle the two crabs that are exactly the same.

Trace the jellyfish.

Draw a jellyfish.

UNDERSEA CUTOUTS

Cut out the undersea ruins and ocean animal pieces. Fold the paper on the lines to make the pieces stand up. Use the pieces to tell a story using the words **first**, **then**, **next**, and **last**.

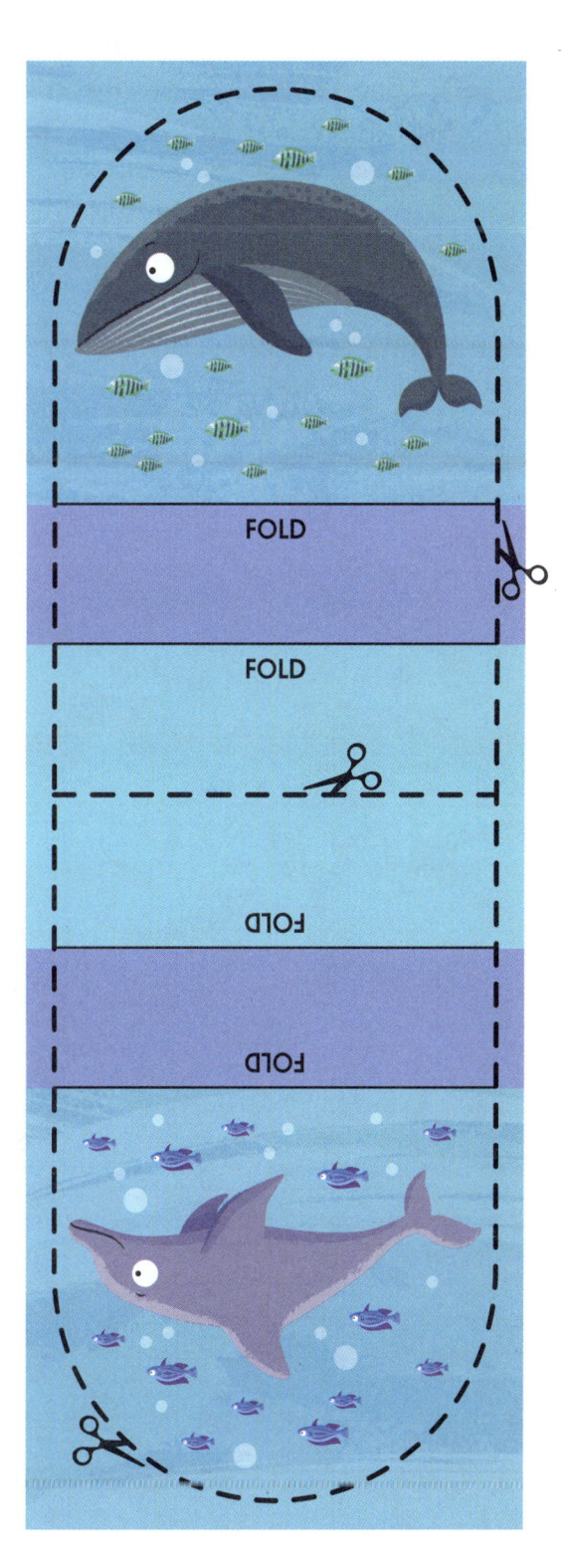

FOLD

FOLD

FOLD

FOLD

FOLD

FOLD

191

MONSIEUR SEAHORSE

Connect the dots from 1–25.
Color the picture.

193

DOLPHIN CALF'S DARING DIVE

Draw a line from the dolphin calf to the dolphin.

NAME THE SEA ANIMAL

Write the beginning letter for each sea animal.

_____ ctopus

_____ rab

_____ olphin

_____ ellyfish

195

OCEAN CRITTERS

Color one box for each animal or seashell you see in the picture below.

	1	2	3	4	5	6	7	8	9	10
Snails										
Crabs										
Seahorses										
Seashells										

CRABTASTIC!

Cut out the puzzle pieces and mix them up.
Put the puzzle pieces together.

5   6   7   8   9   10

197

THE GREAT BLUE WHALE

Connect the dots from 1-30.
Color the picture.

199

OCEAN PARTY!

Find and circle the hidden pictures.

| Find 1 jellyfish | Find 5 clams | Find 1 manta ray | Find 2 sea anemones | Find 4 sharks | Find 3 crabs |

OCEANNA OCTOPUS

Connect the dots from 1–30.
Color the picture.

201

LEARN TO DRAW

Follow the steps to draw sea turtles and fish.

Step 1:
Draw a **half-circle** for the top shell.

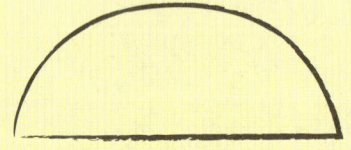

Step 2:
Draw a line for the head.

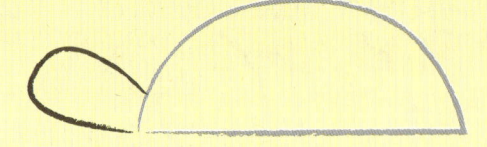

Step 3:
Draw two **half-circles** for the flippers.

Step 4:
Draw a **dot** for the eyes and lines for the mouth and bottom shell.

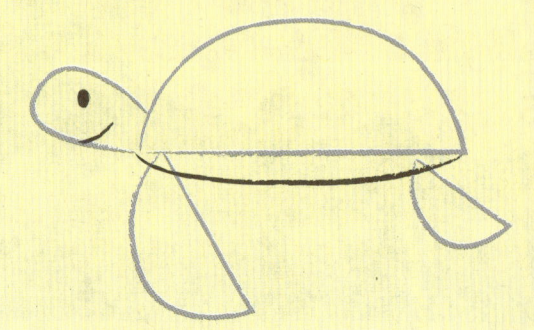

Step 1:
Draw an **oval** for the body.

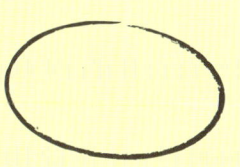

Step 2:
Draw a **half-circle** for the tail.

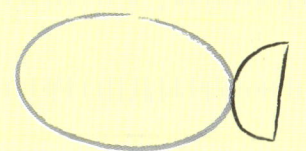

Step 3:
Draw lines for the gills and top fin.

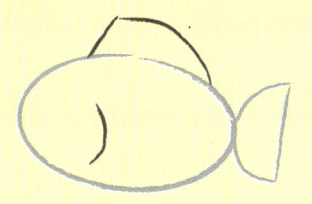

Step 4:
Draw a **dot** for the eye and lines for the mouth and fins.

TAG WITH MR. NIBBLES

Connect the dots from 1–30.
Color the picture.

204

SEA TURTLES

Find and circle the two sea turtles that are exactly the same.

Trace the drawing of the sea turtle. Color the picture.

205

SEA OTTER EXPLORES

Follow the directions to color the picture.

Color the otter **brown**

Color these fish **yellow**

Color these fish **red**

Color the clams **orange**

Color the starfish **pink**

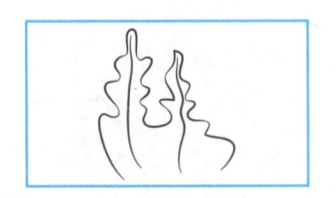

Color the seaweed **green**

206

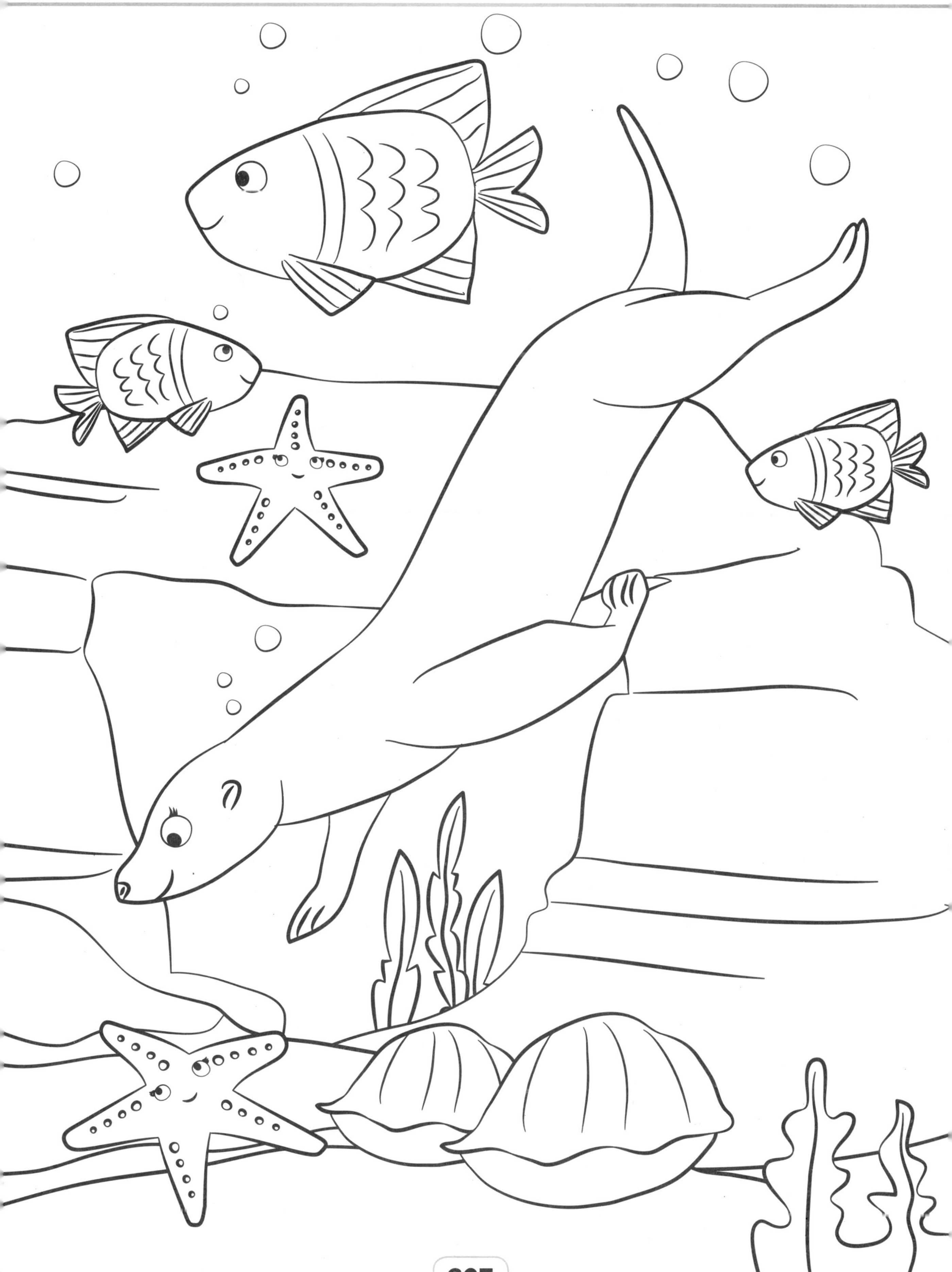

GRAND GOLDFISH

Color the picture.

● = orange   ● = green   ● = pink
● = yellow   ● = purple

RIDDLE ME THIS

Solve the addition and subtraction problems.
Use the code to solve the riddle below.

A: 10 − 1 =
L: 2 + 8 =
D: 3 + 4 =

I: 1 − 1 =
G: 5 + 0 =

O: 7 − 3 =
H: 10 − 2 =

S: 4 − 1 =
F: 2 + 4 =

What kind of fish costs the most?

| 9 | 5 | 4 | 10 | 7 | 6 | 0 | 3 | 8 |

DESERT TREK

Find the pictures below, and then check the box next to the picture.

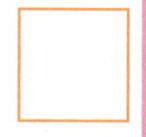

☐  1 coyote ☐  2 rabbits ☐  3 blue jays ☐  4 chipmunks

210

LIZARD LABYRINTH

Draw a line from the ➡ to the **End**.

OMNIVOROUS ARMADILLO

Connect the dots from 1–30.
Color the picture.

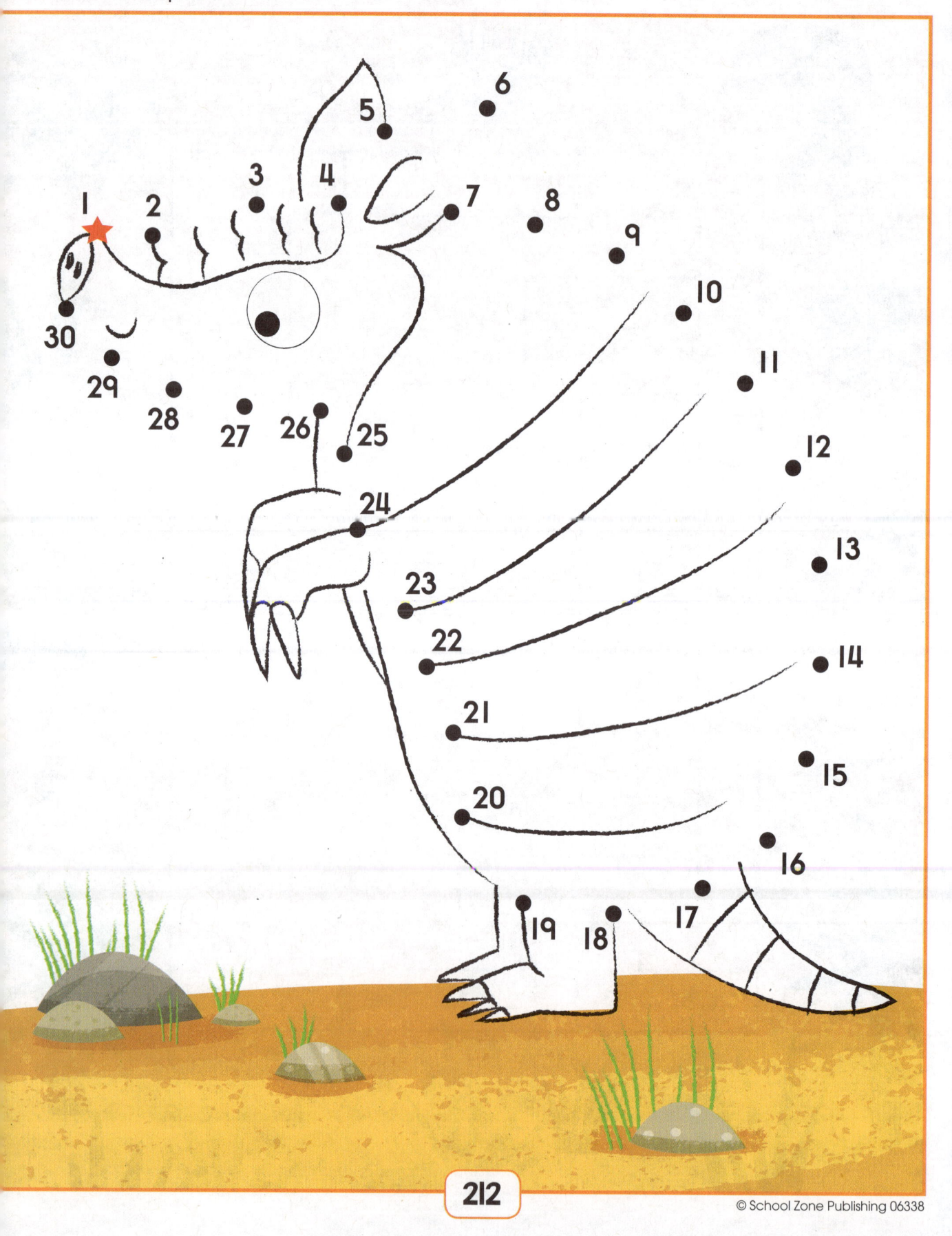

212

MEERKAT HABITAT

Find and circle all of the 🦫's in the picture.

CAMEL SHADOWS

Draw a line from each camel to its shadow.

214

ROADRUNNER'S RACE

Draw a line from the ➡ to the **End**.

Add. How many are there in all?

3 + 7 = ___

6 + 2 = ___

215

IRIDESCENT SCARAB

Color the picture.

- ● = orange
- ● = brown
- ● = dark blue
- ● = green
- ● = purple

216

RESTING CAMELS

Cut out the puzzle pieces and mix them up.
Put the puzzle pieces together.

217

218

CORN SNAKE CUTOUT

Cut out the snake.

MOUNTAIN GOAT

Connect the dots from 1–30.
Color the picture.

DESERT LIFE

Find the pictures below, and then check the box next to each picture. Color each picture.

☐ 3 lizards

☐ 1 rattlesnake

☐ 3 owls

☐ 4 cactuses

☐ 1 roadrunner

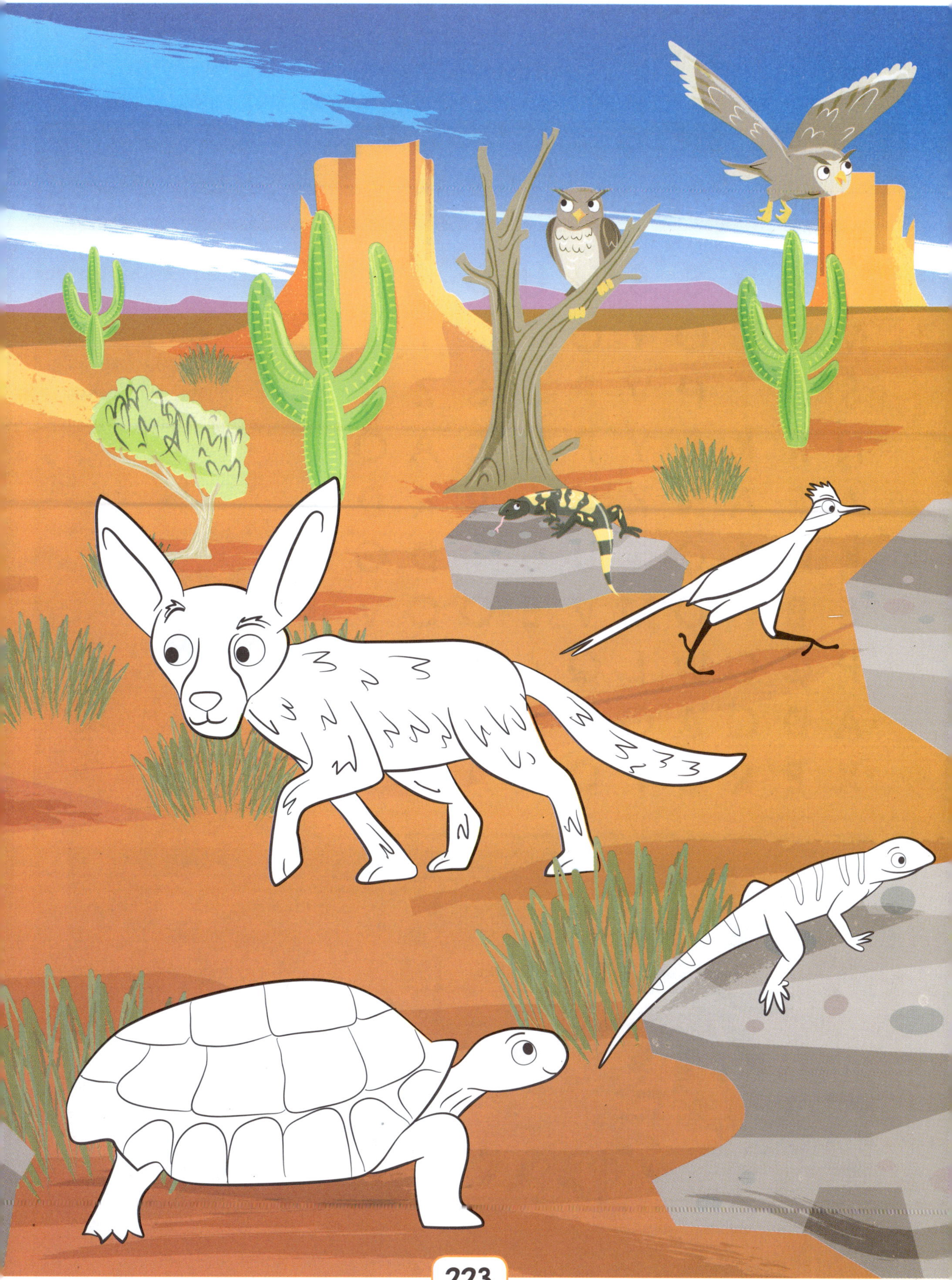

TAWNY'S CACTUS PERCH

Look at the word list.
Circle the words in the puzzle.

COYOTE   OWL   SNAKE   CACTUS   DESERT   FOX   LIZARD

```
B Z V S S H U D L T
M R C O Y O T E I J
S O T H V P J S Z R
N R K E Y P U E A O
A F A N K V L R R D
K C A C T U S T D G
E B W O M V E O O V
P G O W L Q A W N A
A D Q A O E A J S H
X E R O F O X A U F
```

224

SLITHER IN THE SAND

Connect the dots from 1–30.
Color the picture.

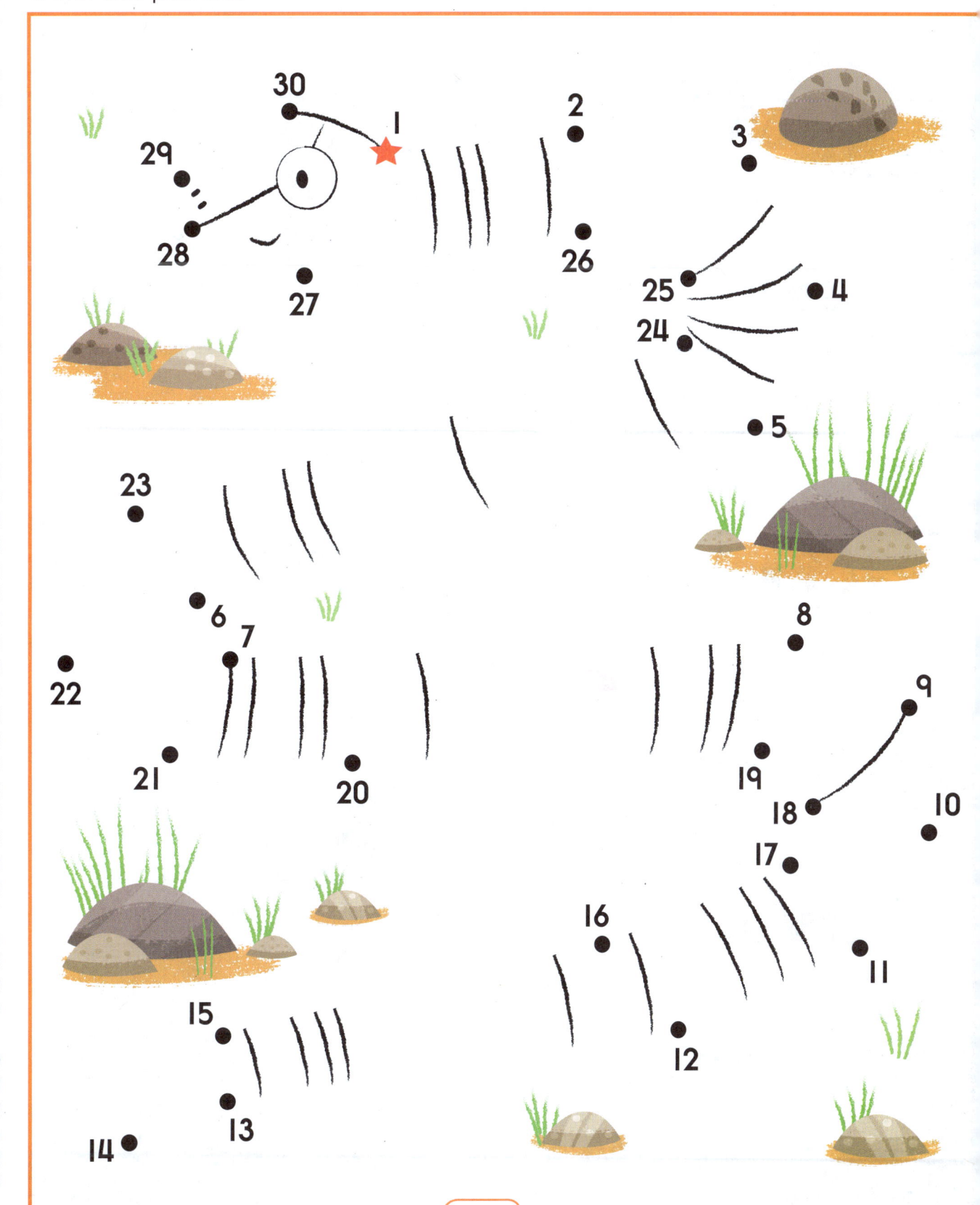

225

WHAT'S DIFFERENT?

Find and circle **9** things that are different in **picture A** and **picture B**.

Picture A

Picture B

226

RIVER LIFE CUTOUTS

Cut out the river and animal pieces. Fold the paper on the lines to make the pieces stand up. Use the pieces to tell a story using the words **first**, **then**, **next**, and **last**.

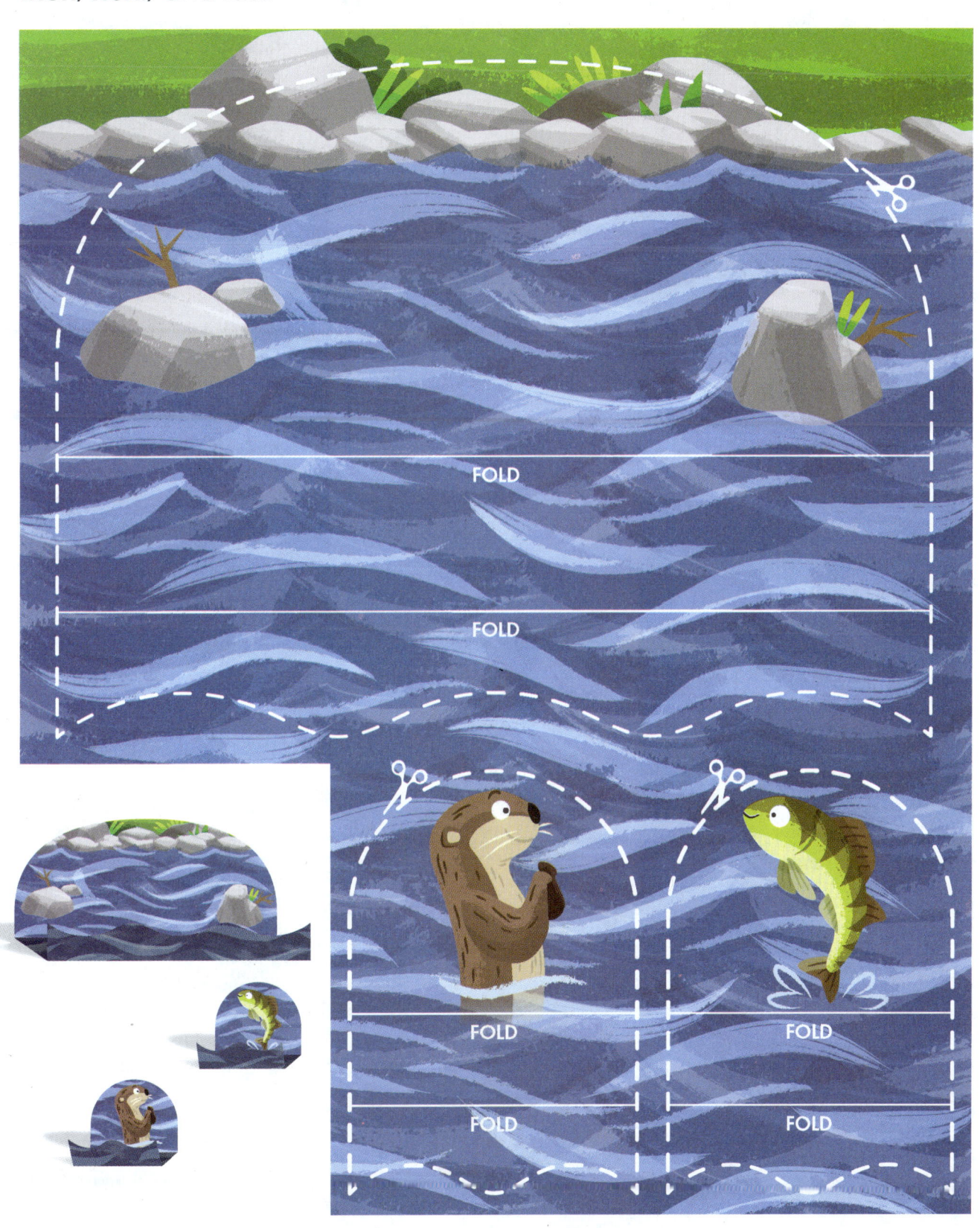

227

228

RIVER OTTER'S LUNCH

Draw a line from the ➡ to the **End**.

End

229

RAIN FOREST RIVER RIDE

Find the pictures below, and then check the box next to the picture. Color the animals.

☐ 1 tiger

☐ 2 snakes

☐ 3 gibbons

☐ 1 elephant

☐ 4 parrots

231

TOUCAN OVERLOOK

Find and circle the hidden pictures.

| iguana |  monkey |  butterfly |  toucan |  insect |  parrot |

232

BLUE MACAW MEETUP

Draw a line from the ➡ to the **End**.

233

COLORFUL TOUCAN

Color the picture.

● = yellow   ● = black   ● = orange
● = red   ● = blue   ● = dark green

234
© School Zone Publishing 06338

JUNGLE CAT

Cut out the puzzle pieces and mix them up.
Put the puzzle pieces together.

235

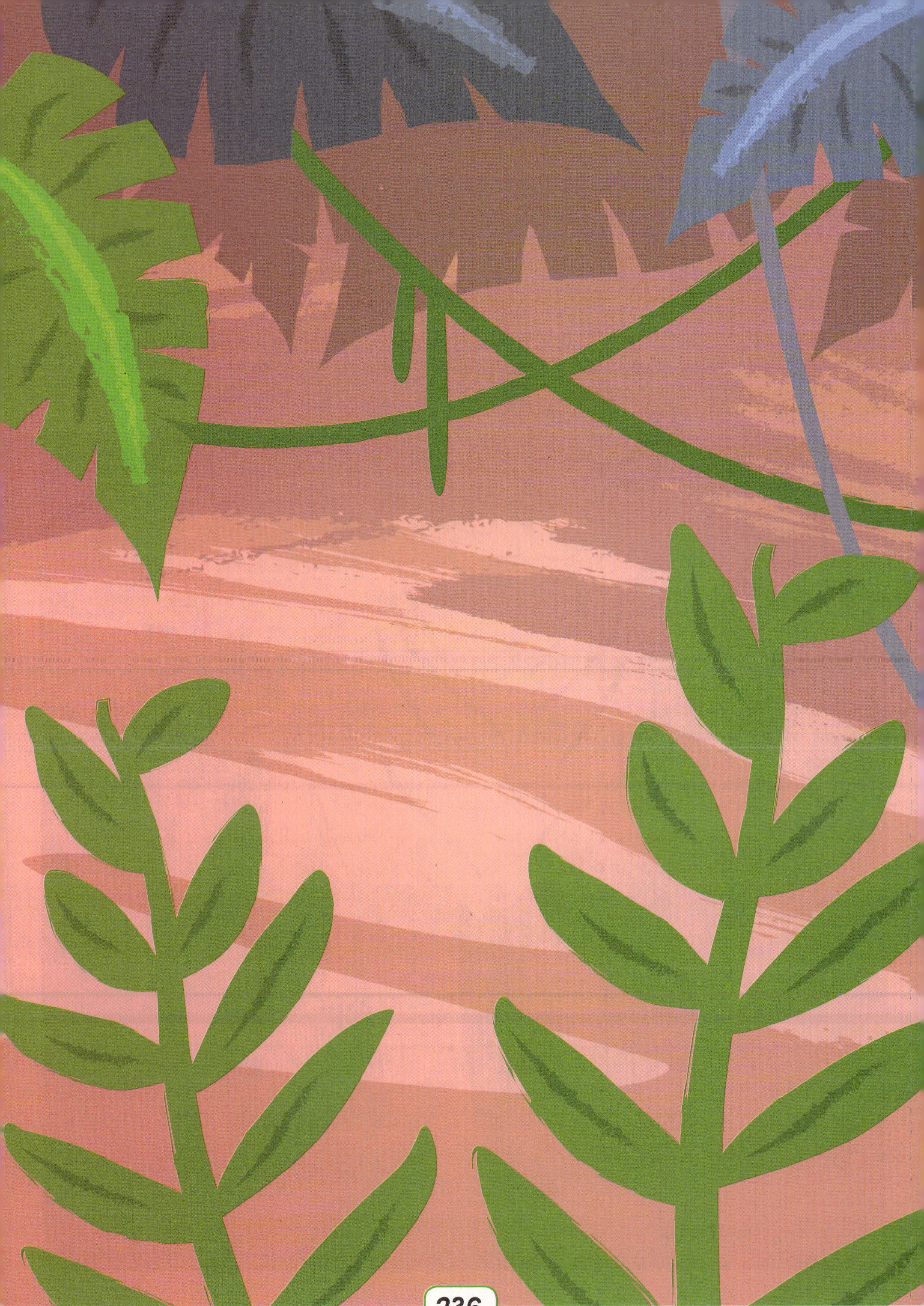

HOWLING FOR STAR FRUIT

Draw a line from the ➡ to the End.

Trace the howler monkey.

Draw a howler monkey.

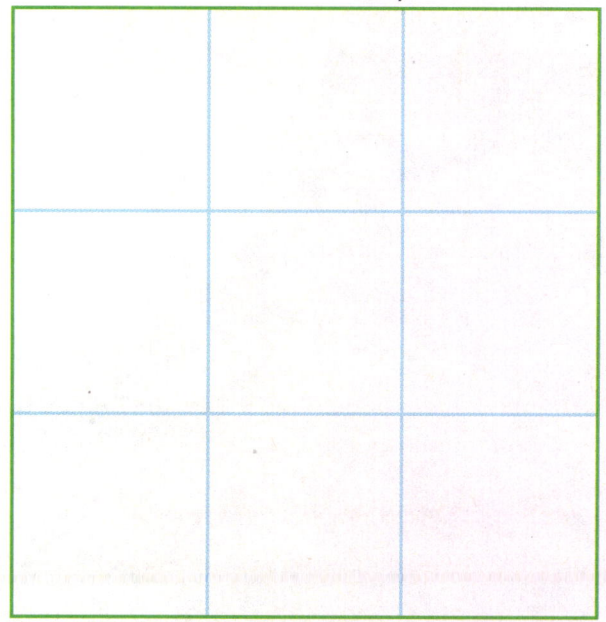

237

MANTIS SPIES HER LUNCH

Draw a line from the ➡ to the **End**.

ORANGUTAN HANG TIME

Cut out the puzzle pieces and mix them up.
Put the puzzle pieces together.

239

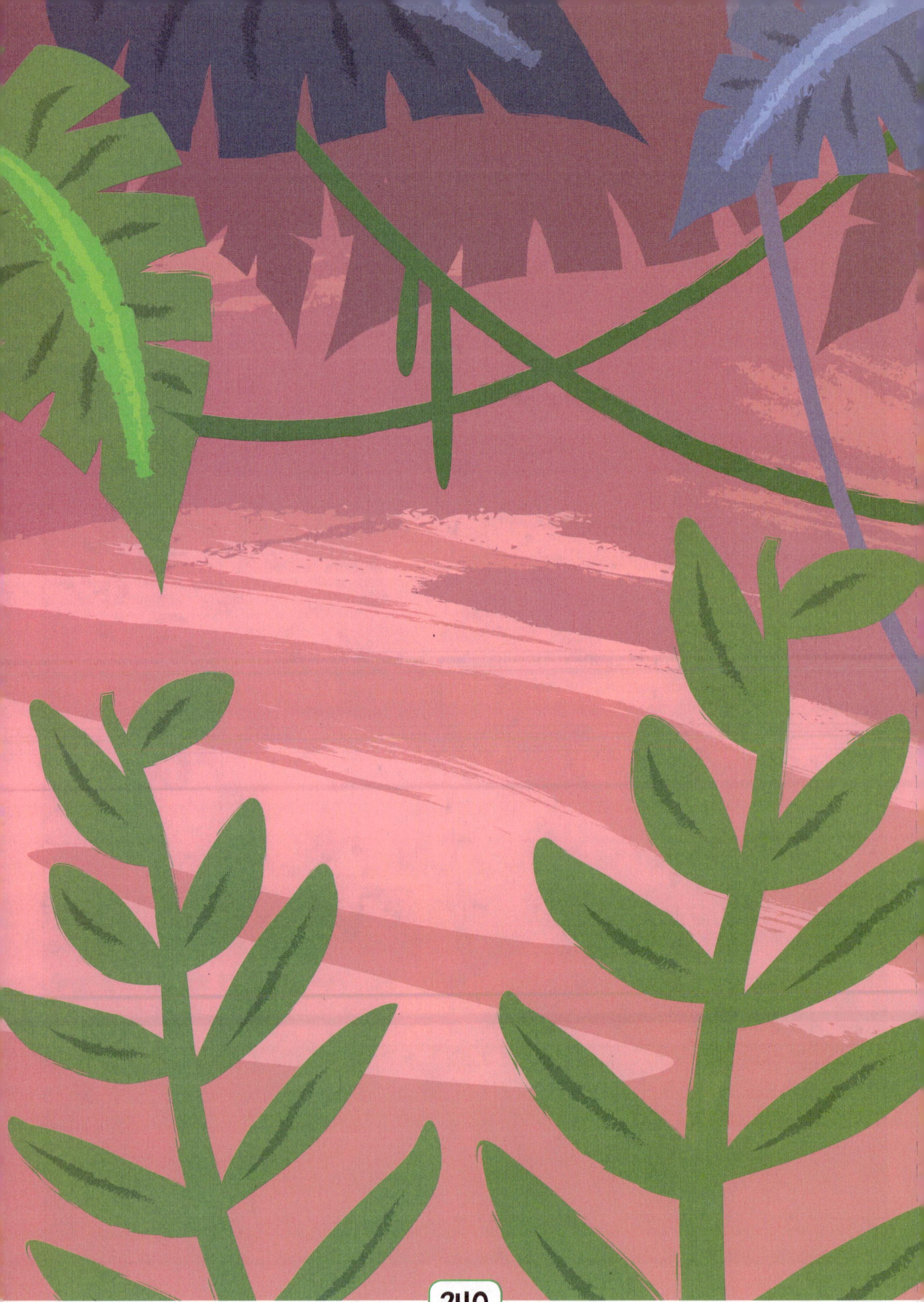

POLLY PARROT PERCHED

Color the picture.

- ● = yellow
- ● = black
- ● = purple
- ● = blue
- ● = gray
- ● = green
- ● = brown
- ● = red

241

WHAT'S DIFFERENT?

Find and circle **6** things that are different in **picture A** and **picture B**.

Picture A

Picture B

RAIN FOREST BUTTERFLIES

Color the picture.

- ● = blue
- ● = purple
- ● = pink
- ● = orange
- ● = yellow
- ● = brown

243

LEARN TO DRAW

Step 1: Draw a **circle** for the head.

Step 2: Draw **circles** on the face and an **oval** for the body.

Step 3: Draw **circles** for the ears, a **triangle** for the nose, and a line for the tail.

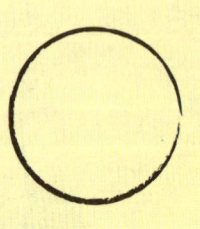

Follow the steps to draw pandas.

244

Step 4:
Draw **circles** and **dots** for the eyes and lines for the mouth, stripes and legs.

Step 5:
Color the black areas.

SLITHERING VINES

Draw a line from the ➡ to the **End**.

246

End

247

CHIMPANZEE PARADISE

Find and circle the hidden pictures.

| chimpanzee |  banana |  plant |  insect |  parrot |  snail |

248

WHAT'S DIFFERENT?

Find and circle **6** things that are different in **picture A** and **picture B**.

Picture A

Picture B

249

A LIVELY RAIN FOREST

Follow the directions to color the picture below.

Color the frog green.

Color the cockatoo yellow.

Color the hibiscus pink.

Color the spider blue.

Color the snake brown.

Color the sloth gray.

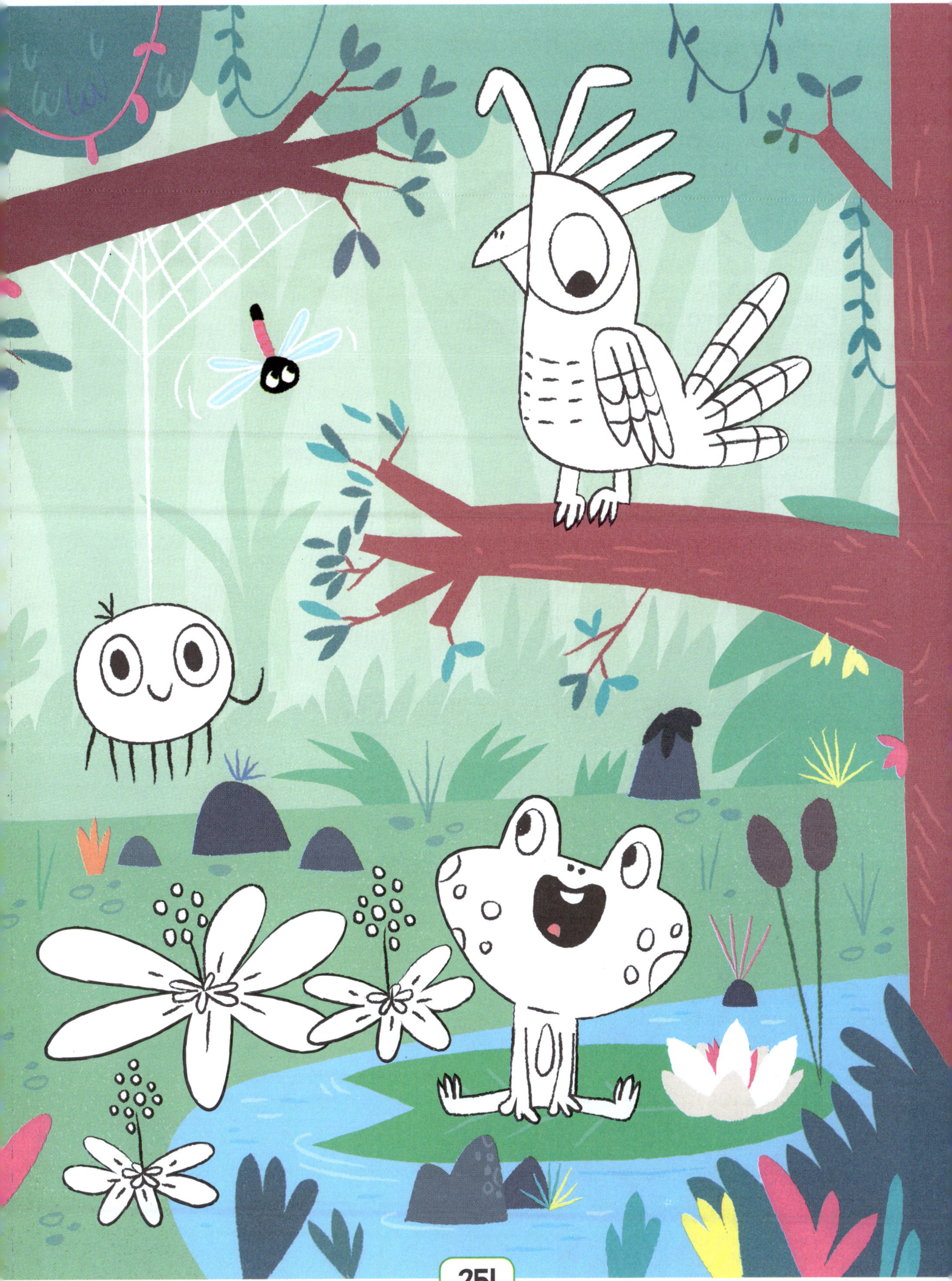

LEARN TO DRAW

Step 1:
Draw an **oval** for the body.

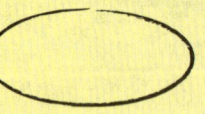

Step 2:
Draw an **oval** for the head and two lines for the tail.

Step 3:
Draw lines for the legs.

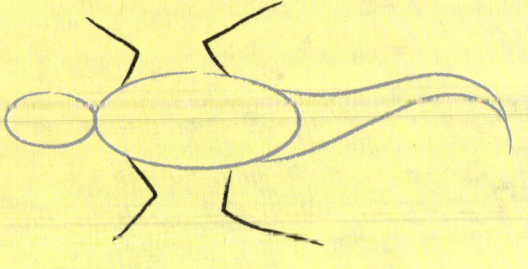

Step 4:
Draw lines for the toes and cheeks.

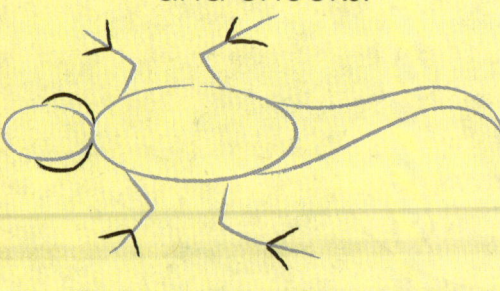

Step 5:
Draw **dots** for the eyes and **circles** for the toes.

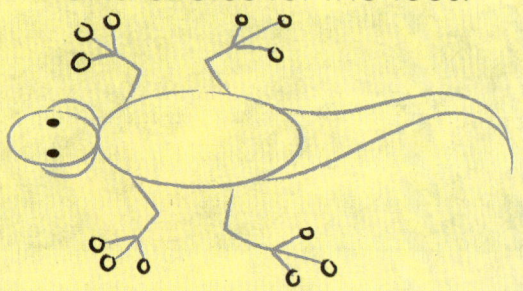

Follow the steps to draw lizards and snakes.

252

© School Zone Publishing 06338

Step 1:
Draw a curvy line for the body.

Step 2:
Draw another curvy line to finish the body.

Step 3:
Draw an **oval** for the head.

Step 4:
Draw a **dot** for the eye and two lines for the tongue.

AN ARMY OF FROGS!

Color one box for each animal you see in the picture below.

		1	2	3	4	5	6	7	8	9	10
	Red Frogs										
	Blue Frogs										
	Green Frogs										
	Yellow Frogs										

254

PRECISE PARROTS

Find and circle the two parrots that are exactly the same.

255

DART FROG

Trace the drawing of the dart frog.
Color the picture to match this one:

256

THE LEOPARD'S SPOTS

Color the leopard's spots. Color the picture.

257

CHAMELEONS

Find and circle the picture that matches this one:

ARCTIC CUTOUTS

Cut out the iceberg and animal pieces. Fold the paper on the lines to make the pieces stand up. Use the pieces to tell a story using the words **first**, **then**, **next**, and **last**.

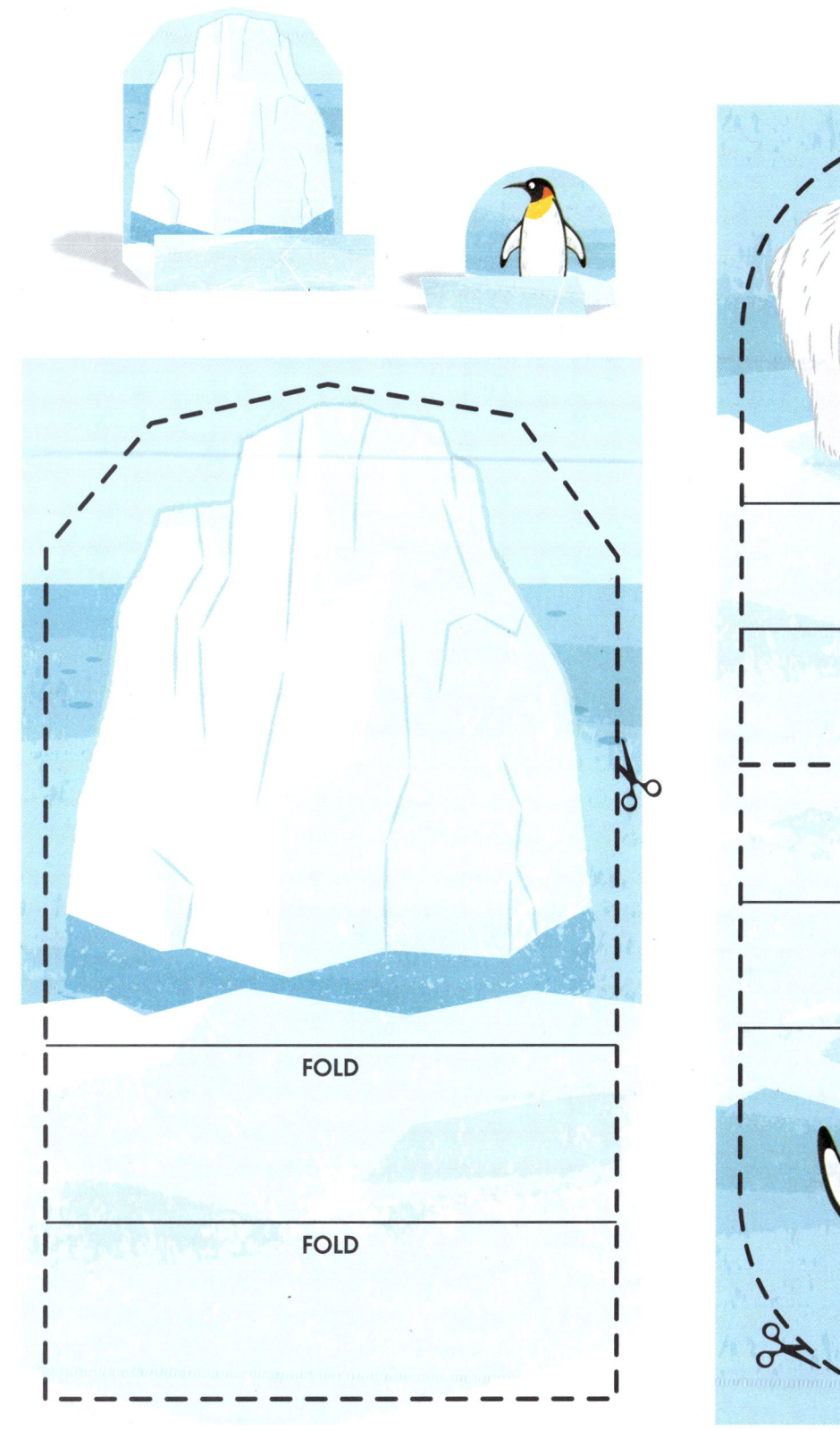

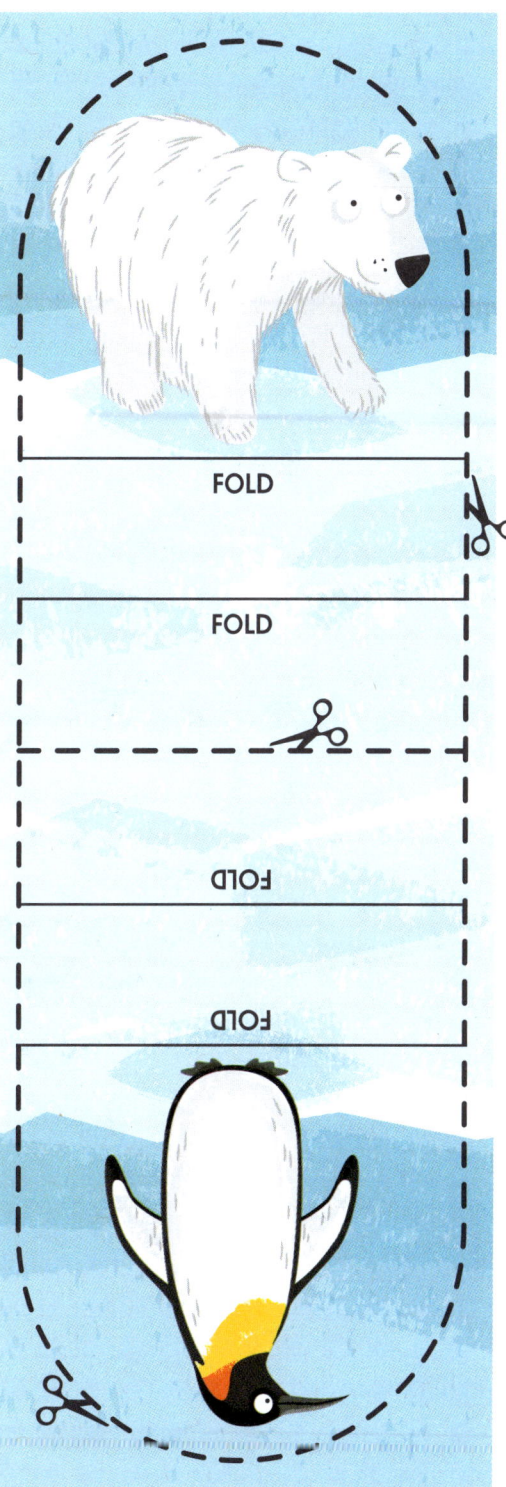

FOLD

FOLD

FOLD

FOLD

FOLD

FOLD

259

CARIBOU

Color the picture.

● = yellow   ● = tan   ● = purple
● = black   ● = gray   ● = brown

261

LOST ON THE ICE FLOES

Draw a line from the ➡ to the **End**.

End

262

ARCTIC OCEAN PALS

Connect the dots from 1–30.
Color the picture.

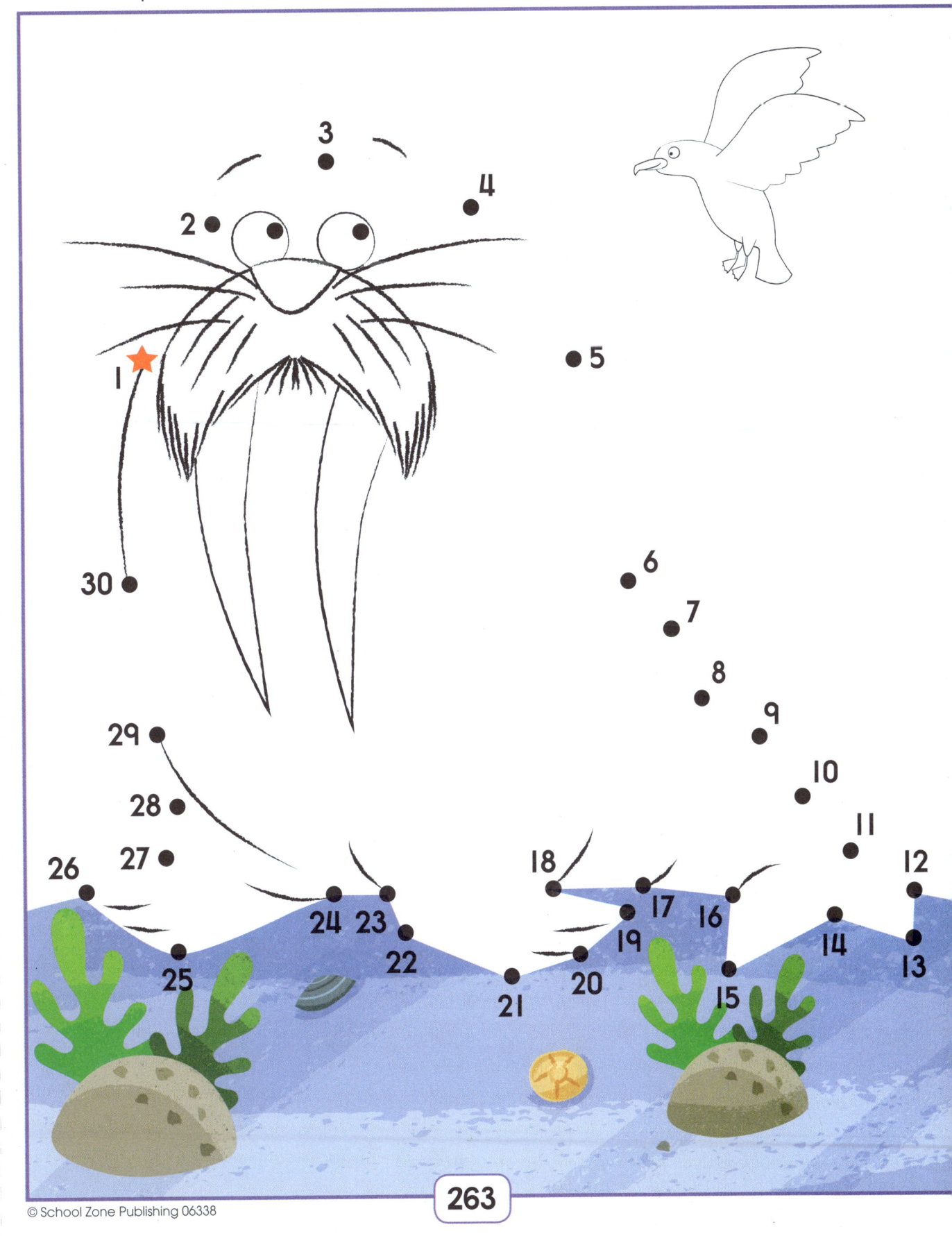

263

WADDLE, WADDLE

Connect the dots from 1–30.
Color the picture.

264

WHAT'S DIFFERENT?

Find and circle **7** things that are different in **picture A** and **picture B**.

Picture A

Picture B

265

MARSH FRIENDS

Color the picture.

● = yellow ● = brown ● = purple ● = tan
● = pink ● = green ● = orange

SPOTTED MARSH FROG

Cut out the puzzle pieces and mix them up.
Put the puzzle pieces together.

267

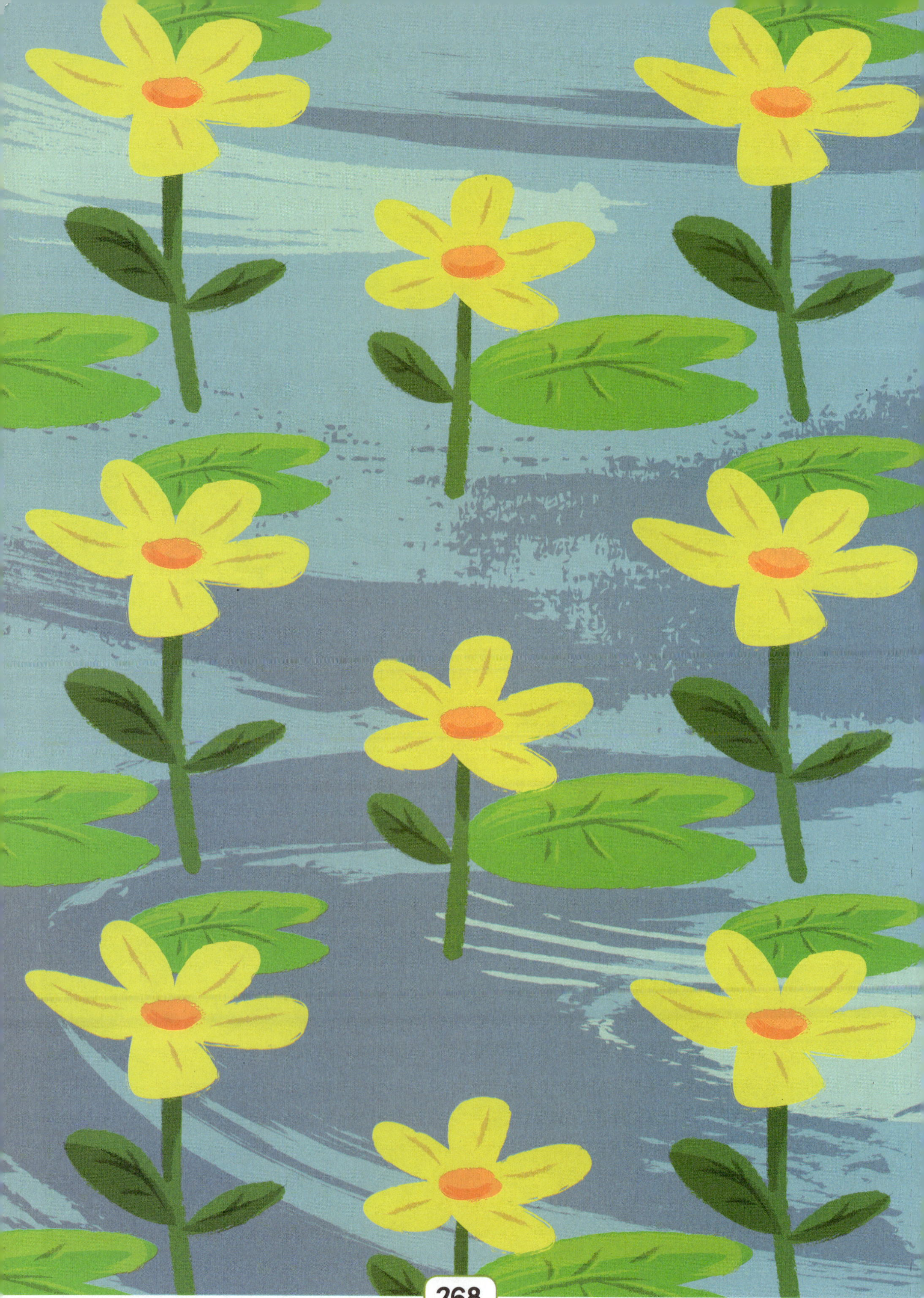

DUCKLING'S RUN

Draw a line from the ➡ to the **End**.

Trace the duckling.

Draw a duckling.

269
© School Zone Publishing 06338

CROCODILE TERRITORY

Find the pictures below, and then check the box next to the picture.

☐ 1 crocodile

☐ 4 baby crocodiles

☐ 1 heron

☐ 4 frogs

☐ 3 turtles

☐ 6 dragonflies

270
© School Zone Publishing 06338

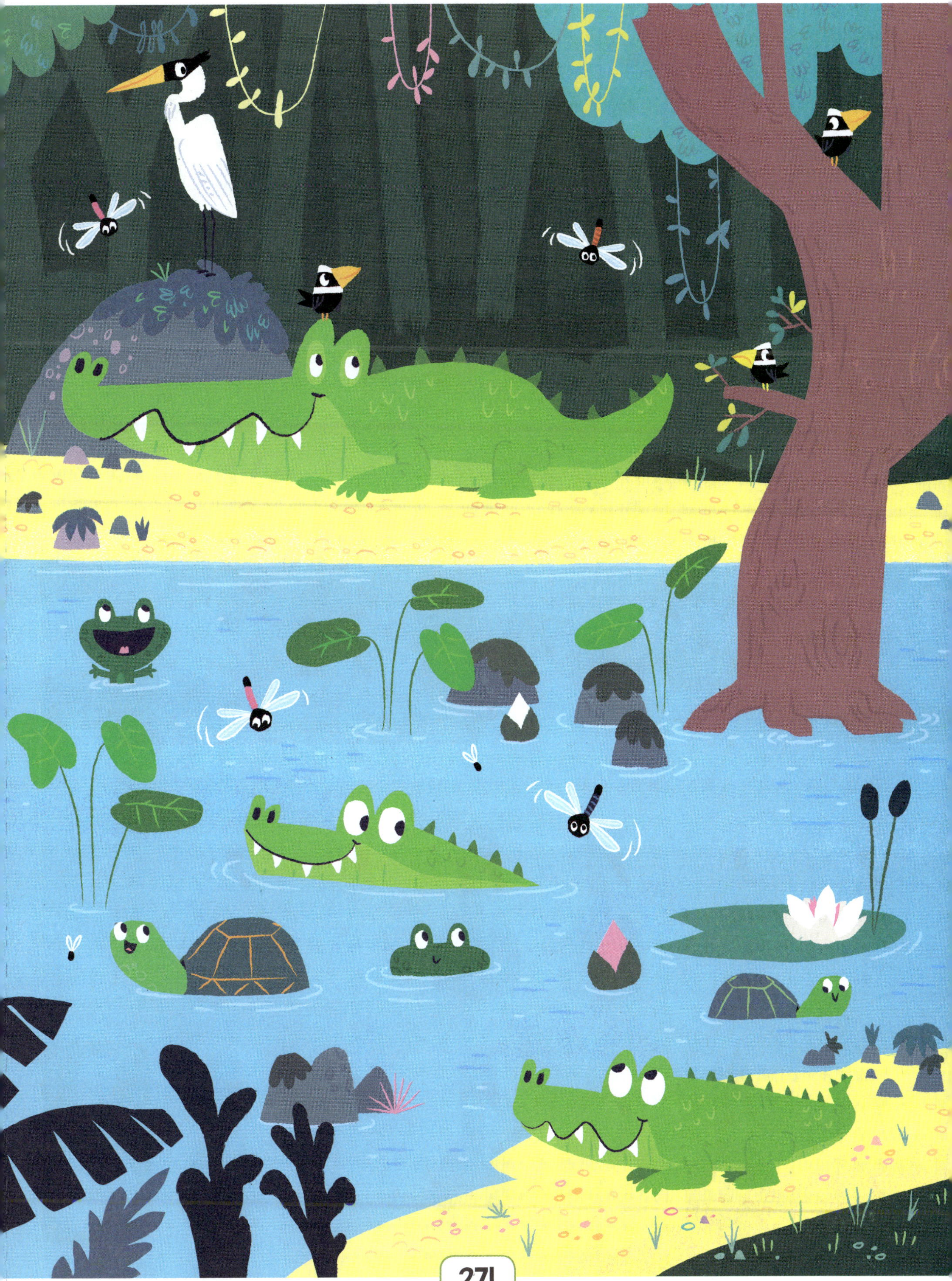

CYBIL SWAN'S CYGNETS

Draw a line from the ➡ to the **End**.

Color the swans to complete the patterns.

BE THE GATOR!

Cut out the alligator mask. Fold the snout up and the teeth down on the fold lines. If you need to, ask for a grown-up's help.

FOLD

FOLD

FOLD

You can also tape a popsicle stick or a straight drinking straw to the back of the mask to make it easier to hold the mask up to your face.

Two more masks can be found in this book:

Lion Mask (page 143)

Zebra Mask (page 155)

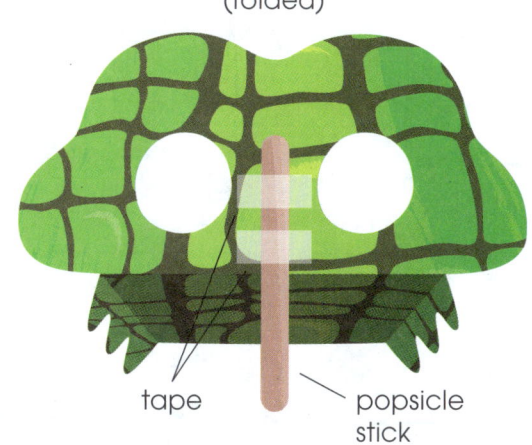

back of mask (folded)

tape

popsicle stick

© School Zone Publishing 06338

273

HIPPETY-HOP!

Connect the dots from 1–30.
Color the picture.

275

LIFE ON THE MARSH

Find and circle the hidden pictures.

| frog | turtle | heron | snake | raccoon | dragonfly |

SCOOTER'S MARSH MOSEY

Connect the dots from 1–30.
Color the picture.

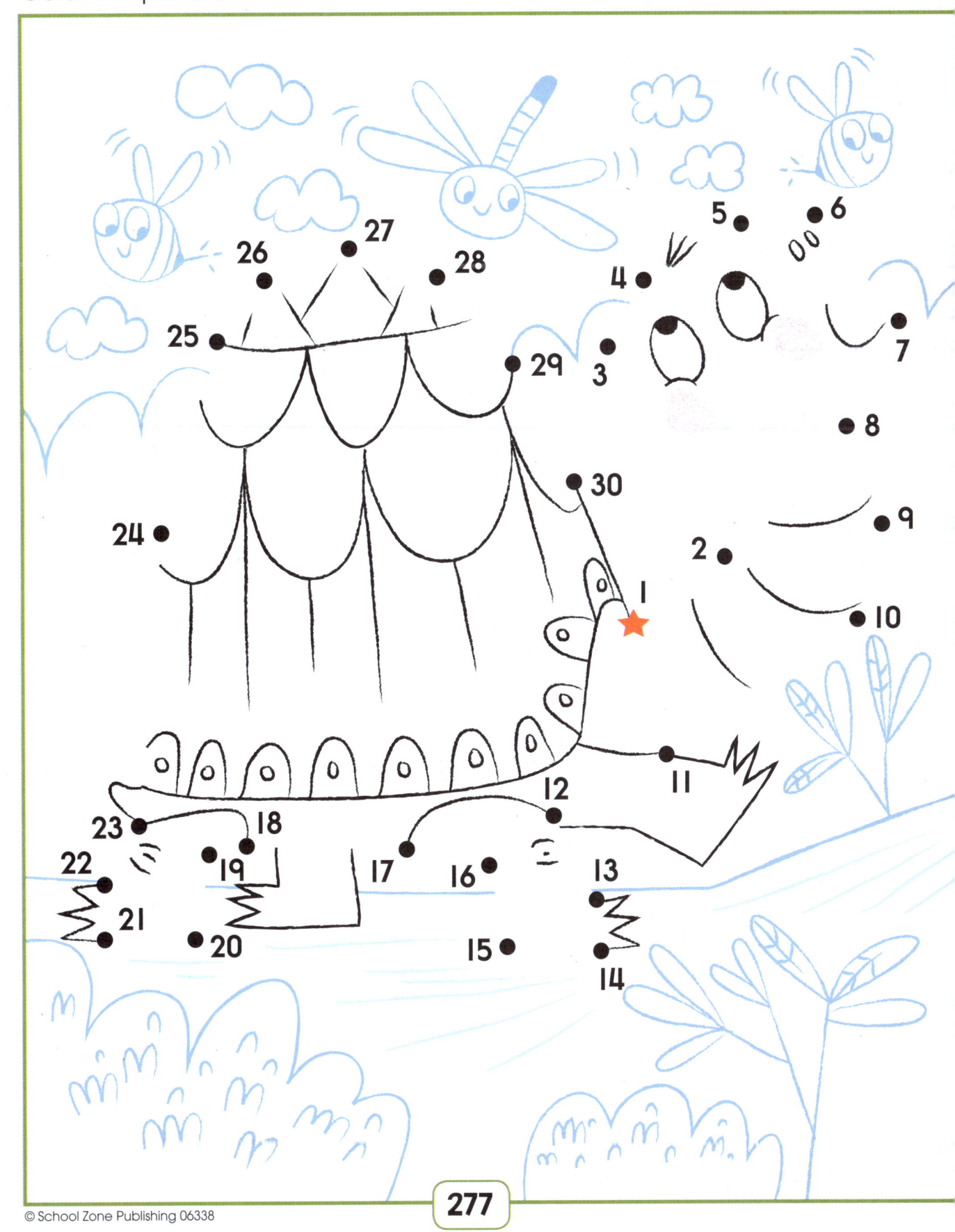

277

GATOR REUNION

Draw a line from the ➡ to the End.

Trace the picture of the alligator.
Color the picture.

278

PLUNGING PLATYPUS

Connect the dots from 1–30.
Color the picture.

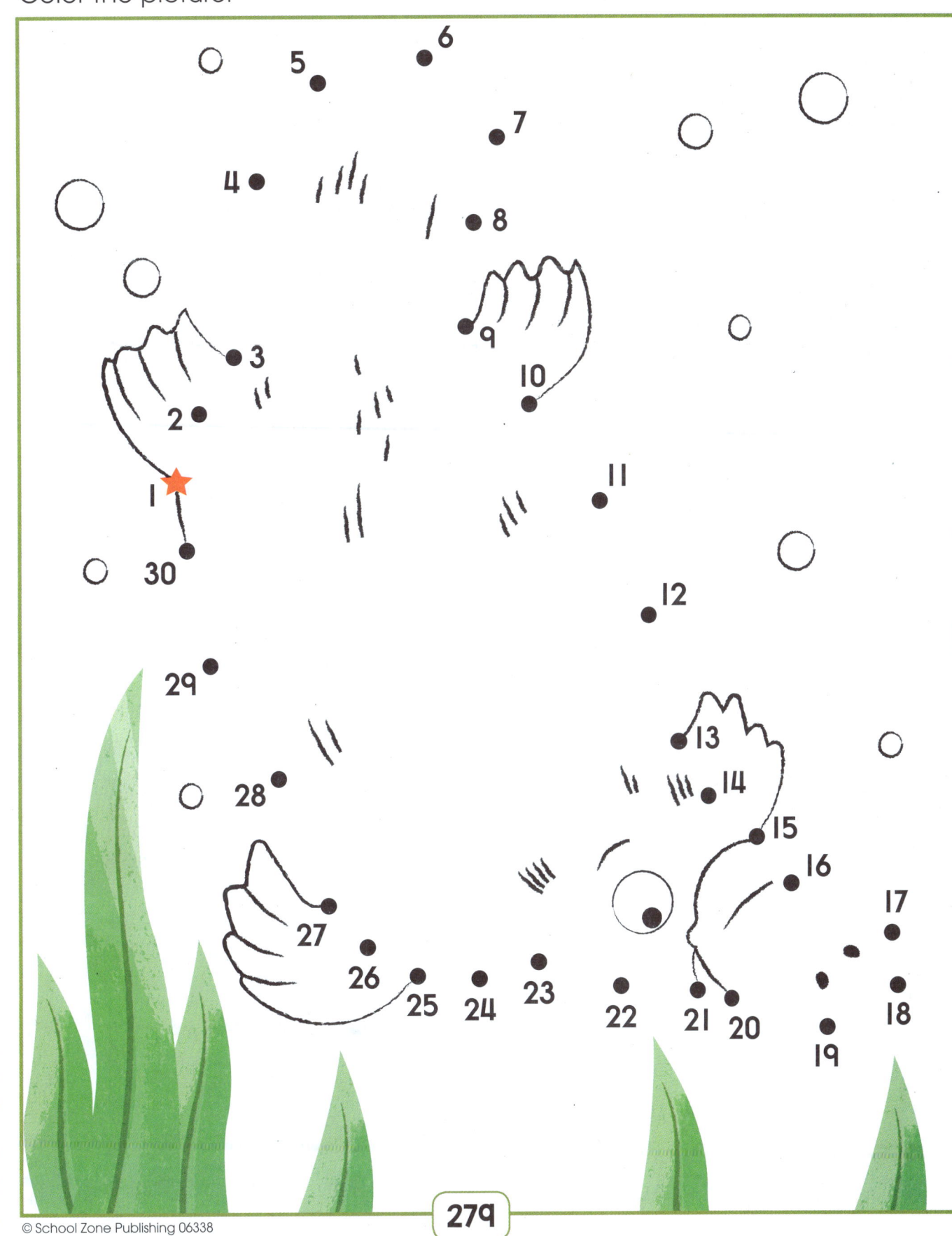

279

LILY PAD TO LILY PAD

Draw a line from the ➡ to the **End**.

End

280

MARSH CUTOUTS

Cut out the marsh and animal pieces. Fold the paper on the lines to make the pieces stand up. Use the pieces to tell a story using the words **first**, **then**, **next**, and **last**.

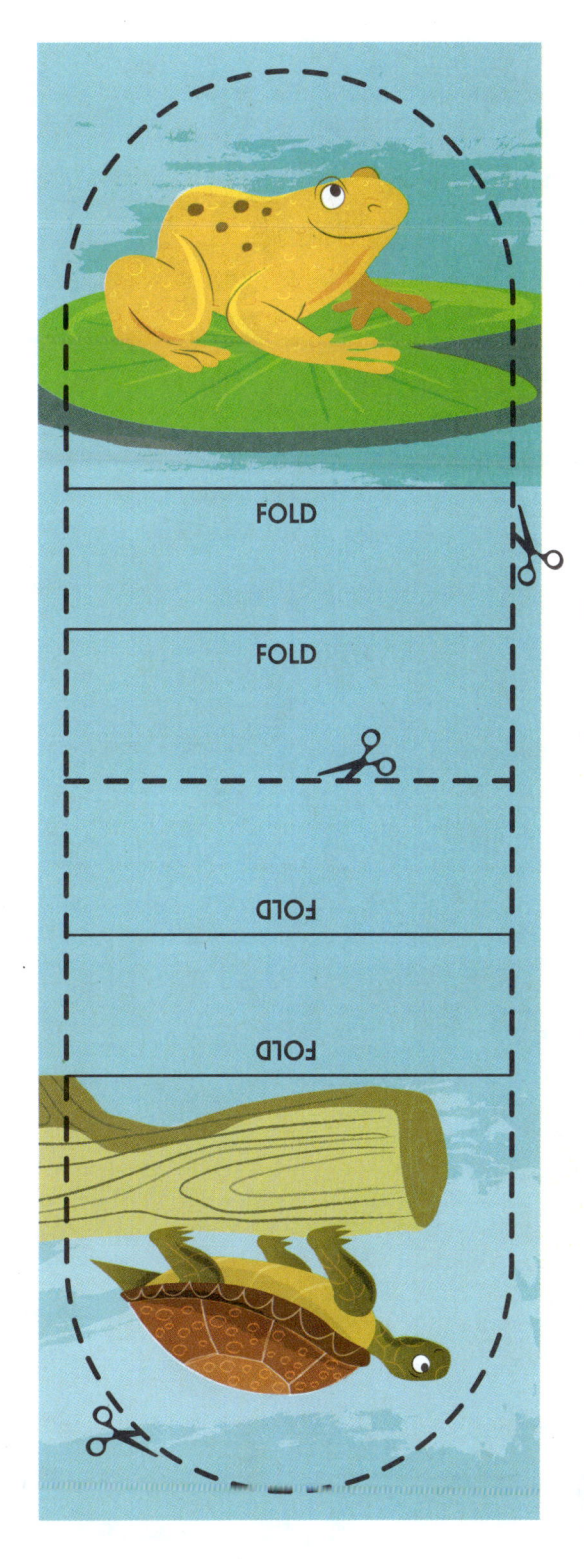

281

282

MARSH MADNESS

Color one box for each animal you see in the picture below.

	1	2	3	4	5	6	7	8	9	10	11	12
Ducks												
Frogs												
Turtles												
Dragonflies												

GENTLE SWAN

Connect the dots from 1–30.
Color the picture.

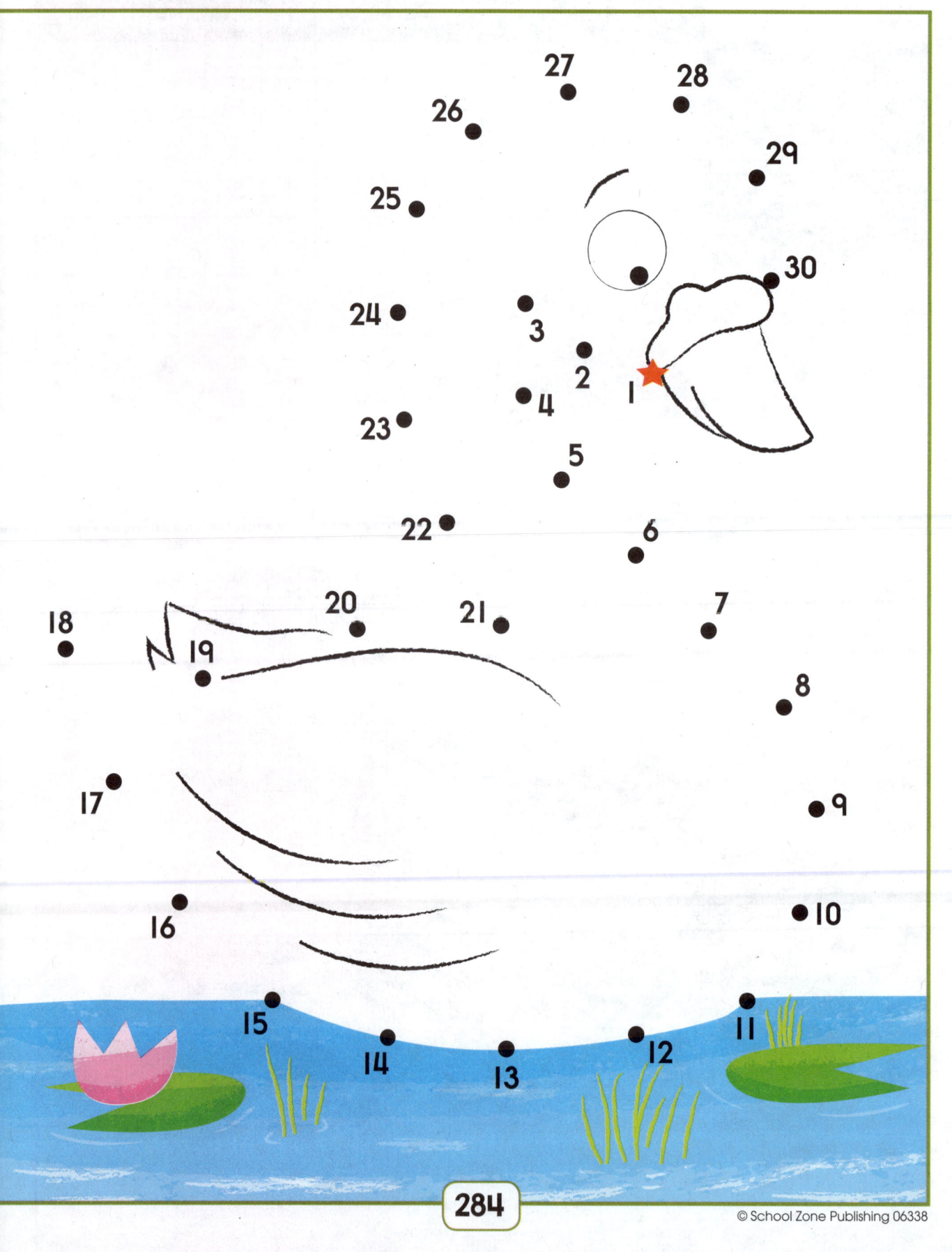

284

ANIMAL CROSSWORD

Use the picture clues to fill in the puzzle.

ants   koala   seal   skunk   octopus

Across
1.
2.
4.

Down
1.
3.

ON THE WAY HOME

Draw a line from each animal to its home.

287

ANIMAL CROSSWORD 2

Use the picture clues to fill in the puzzle.

bear   otter   bird   rhino   deer

Across

1.

3.

5.

Down

2.

4.

5.

288

TYRANT LIZARD KING!

Connect the dots from 1–30.
Color the picture.

289

SOARING PTERANODON

Color the picture.

● = blue   ● = green   ● = red
● = orange   ● = yellow   ● = brown

290

PREHISTORIC CUTOUTS

Cut out the volcano and animal pieces. Fold the paper on the lines to make the pieces stand up. Use the pieces to tell a story using the words **first**, **then**, **next**, and **last**.

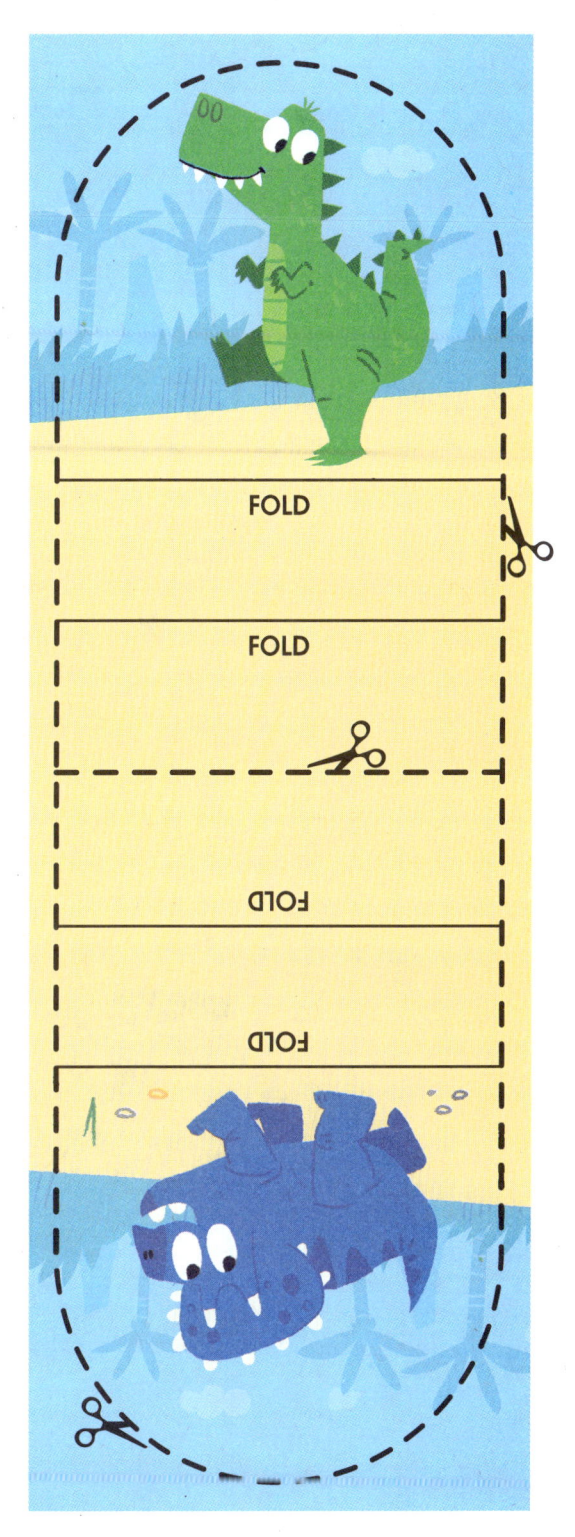

291

292

PLATED STEGOSAURUS

Connect the dots from 1–30.
Color the picture.

293

DINOSAUR SHADOWS

Draw a line from each animal to its shadow.

294

PTERANODON'S NEST

Look at each pattern. Circle what comes next.

PREHISTORIC EGG HUNT

Find and circle the hidden pictures.

| red egg | purple egg | cream egg | blue egg | green egg | yellow egg |

MATCHING DINOS

Find and circle the two dinosaurs that are exactly the same.

297

WHAT'S DIFFERENT?

Find and circle **6** things that are different in **picture A** and **picture B**.

Picture A

Picture B

298
© School Zone Publishing 06338

TRICERATOPS TREK

Cut out the puzzle pieces and mix them up.
Put the puzzle pieces together.

ANSWER KEY

Page 4
Page 5
Page 6
Page 7
Page 8
Page 9
Page 10

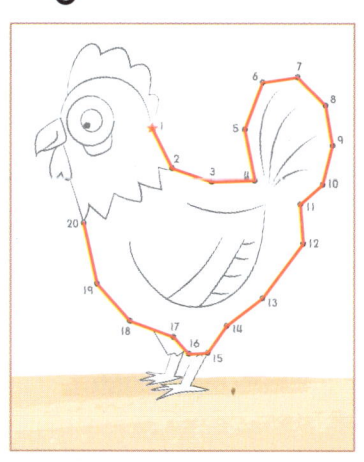

Pig   Horse

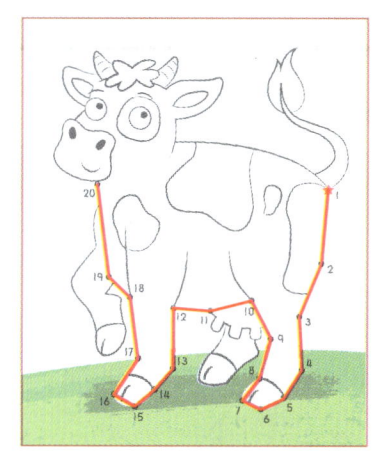

Goat   Cow

Page 11
Pages 12-13

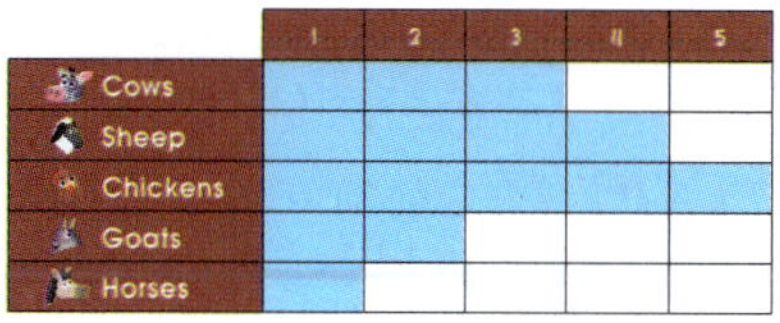

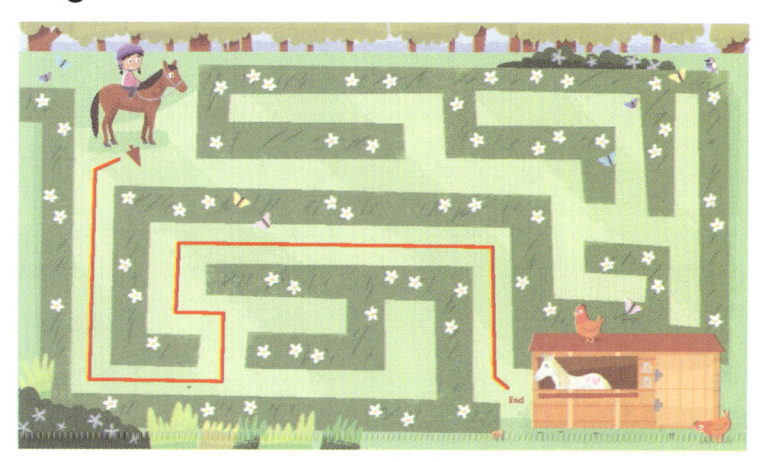

© School Zone Publishing 06338

301

ANSWER KEY

Page 14

Page 15

Page 16

Page 17

Page 18

Page 20

Page 19

A PIGPEN

Page 25

Page 28

Page 30

302

© School Zone Publishing 06338

ANSWER KEY

Page 31

A HORSE

Page 34

Page 35

Page 36

Hawk   Duck
Toucan   Penguin

Page 37

Page 38

Page 39

Page 40

Page 41

Page 42

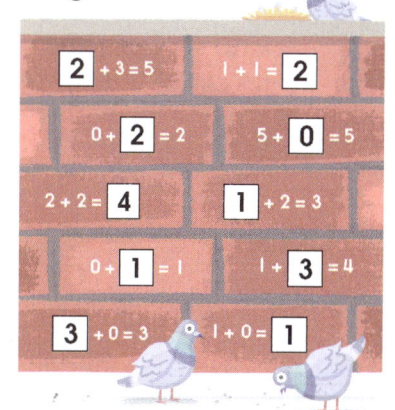

2 + 3 = 5   1 + 1 = 2
0 + 2 = 2   5 + 0 = 5
2 + 2 = 4   1 + 2 = 3
0 + 1 = 1   1 + 3 = 4
3 + 0 = 3   1 + 0 = 1

303

© School Zone Publishing 06338

ANSWER KEY

Page 45

Page 46

Page 49

Pages 52-53

Page 54

Page 55

Page 56

Page 57

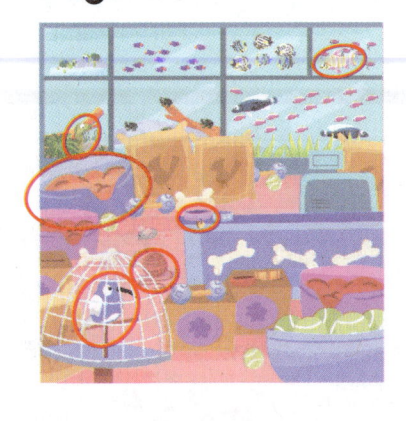

304

© School Zone Publishing 06338

ANSWER KEY

Page 60

Page 61

Page 62

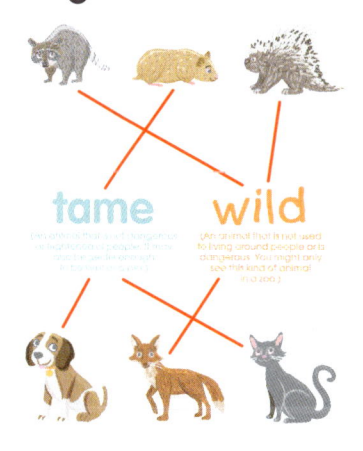

Page 65

Page 66

Page 67

Pages 68-69

Page 70

ANSWER KEY

Page 71

Page 72

Page 73

Pages 74-75

Page 76

1. d o v e
   u
   c
2. h a w k
   e
   r
   o
   n

Page 77

Pages 78-79

FUR

Page 80

Page 81

7 - 5 = 2   4 - 3 = 1

Page 82

306

ANSWER KEY

Page 83

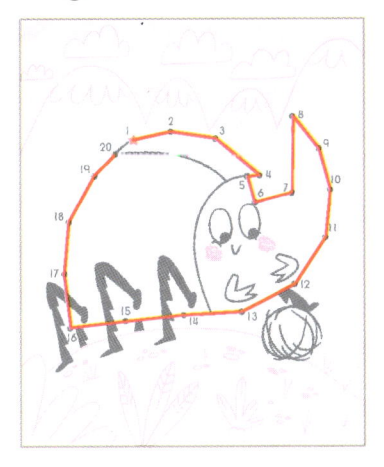

Page 84

Page 85

Pages 86-87

Page 88

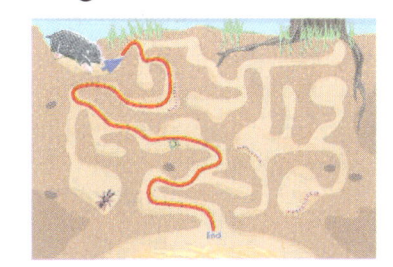

Page 91

Page 92

Page 95

Pages 98-99

307

© School Zone Publishing 06338

ANSWER KEY

Pages 102-103

Page 104

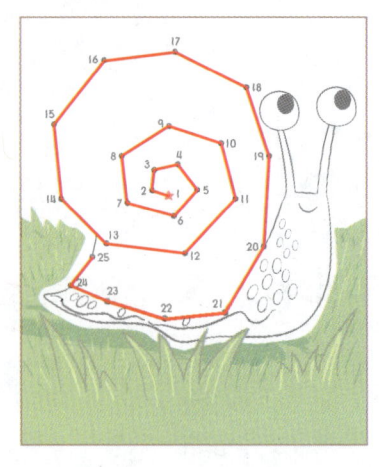

Page 105

Page 106

Page 107

Page 108

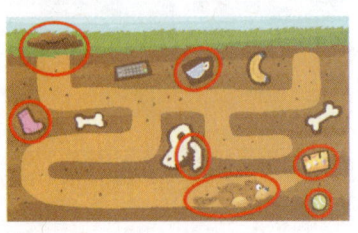

Page 109

Page 110

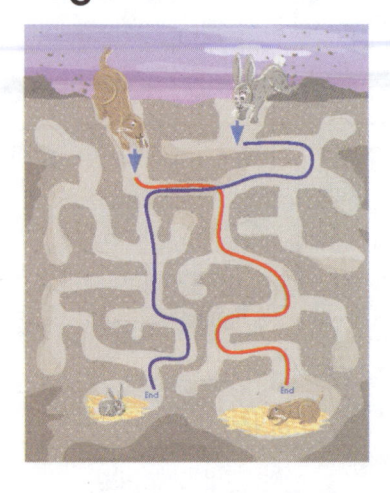

308

© School Zone Publishing 06338

ANSWER KEY

Page 111

Page 112

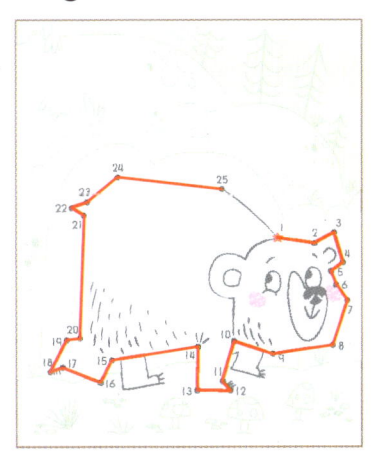

Page 115

Pages 118–119

Pages 120–121

Page 122

Page 125

Page 128

309

© School Zone Publishing 06338

ANSWER KEY

Page 129

Page 130

Page 134

Page 137

Pages 138-139

Page 145

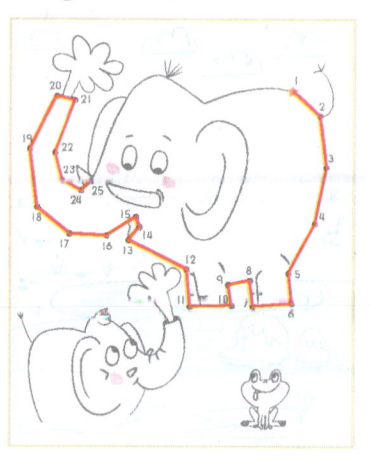

Page 146

Page 149

Page 153

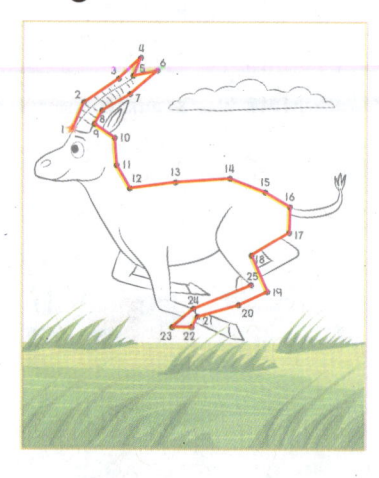

310

© School Zone Publishing 06338

ANSWER KEY

Page 157

Page 158

Page 159

Page 160

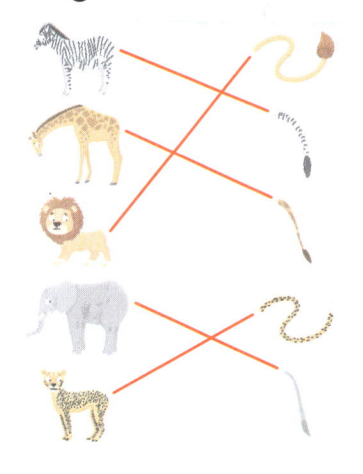

Page 161

Page 164

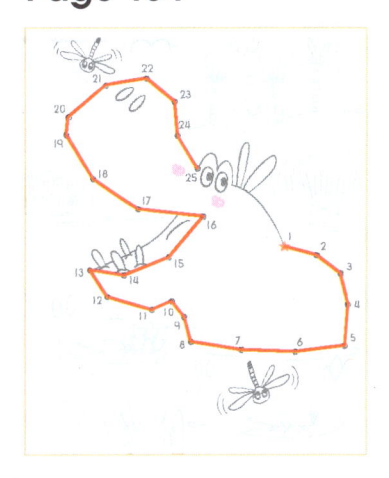

Page 167

Page 168

Page 169

© School Zone Publishing 06338

ANSWER KEY

Page 170

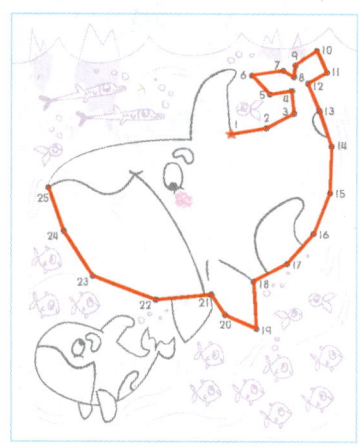

Page 171

Pages 172-173

Page 175

Pages 176-177

Page 178

Page 181

312

© School Zone Publishing 06338

ANSWER KEY

Page 182
Page 183
Page 184
Page 187
Page 190
Page 193
Page 194
Page 195

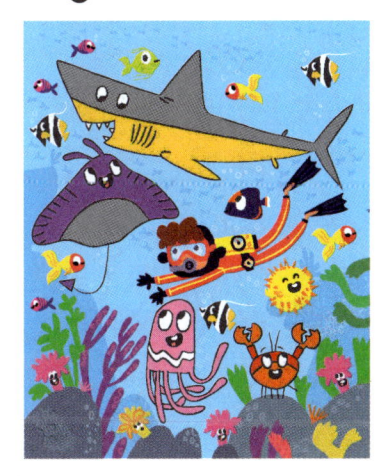

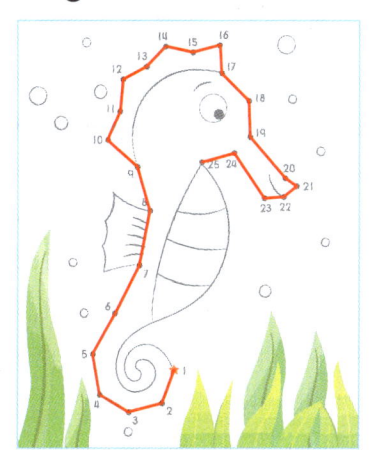

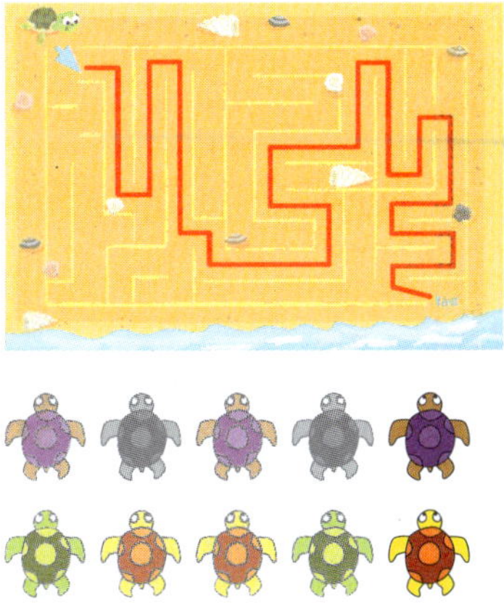

Octopus Crab

Dolphin Jellyfish

Page 196
Page 199

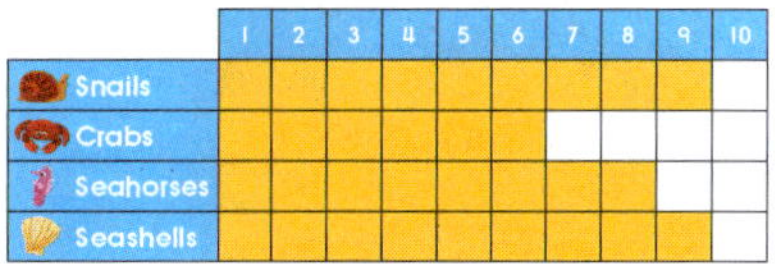

313

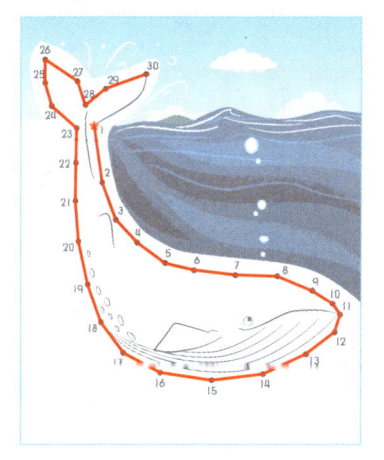

© School Zone Publishing 06338

ANSWER KEY

Page 200

Page 201

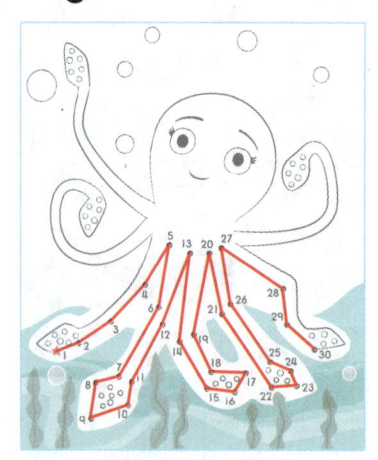

Page 204

Page 205

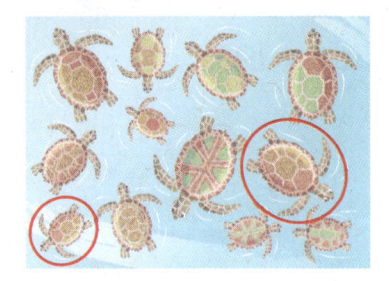

Pages 206-207

Page 208

Page 209 A GOLDFISH

Page 210

Page 211

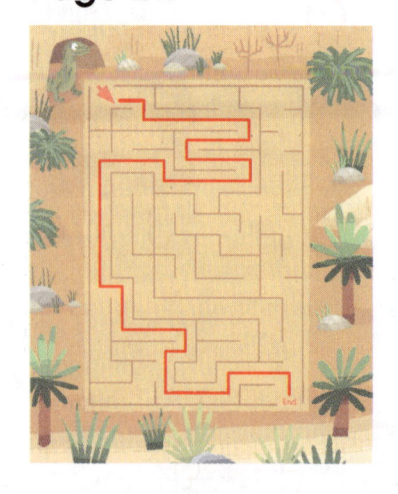

Page 212

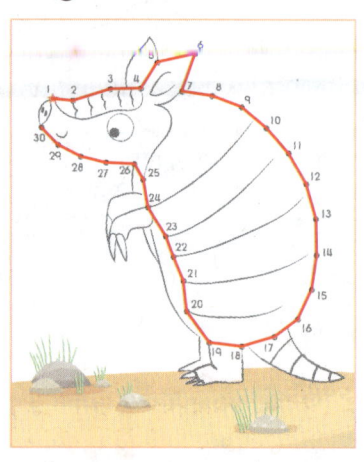

314

© School Zone Publishing 06338

ANSWER KEY

Page 213

Page 214

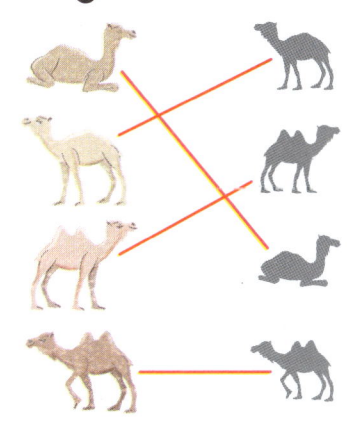

Page 215

3 + 7 = **10**   6 + 2 = **8**

Page 216

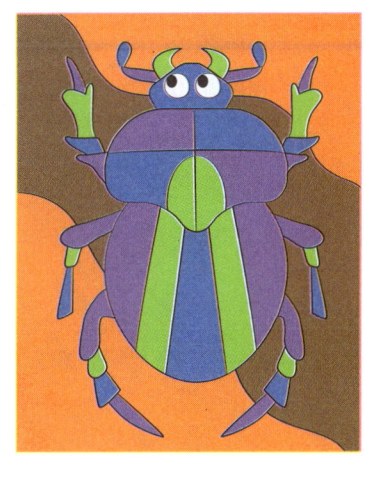

Page 221

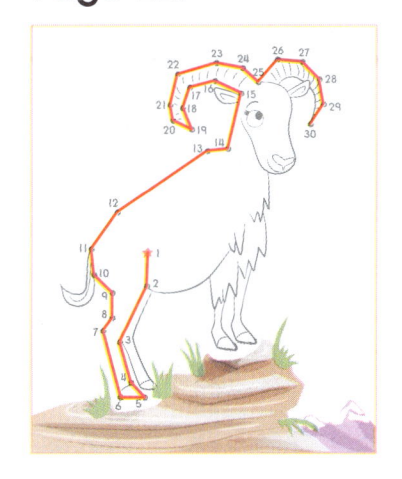

Pages 222–223

Page 224

Page 225

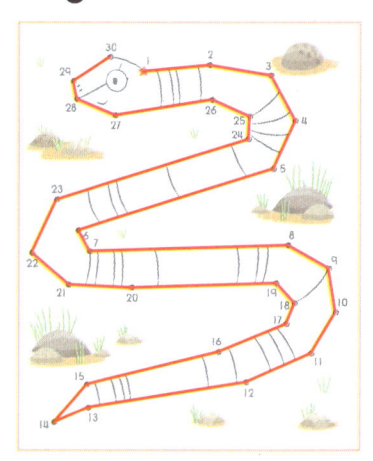

© School Zone Publishing 06338

ANSWER KEY

Page 226

Page 229

Pages 230-231

Page 232

Page 233

Page 234

Page 237

Page 238

Page 241

316

© School Zone Publishing 06338

ANSWER KEY

Page 242

Page 243

Pages 246-247

Page 248

Page 249

Pages 250-251

Page 254

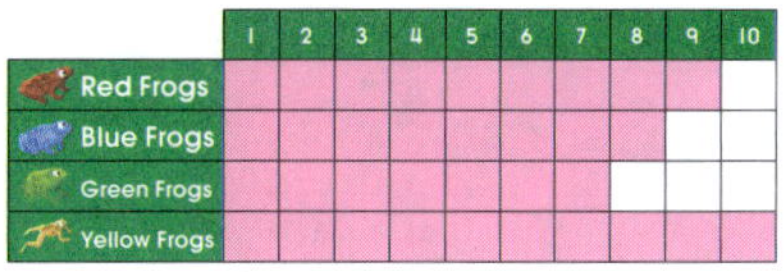

Page 255

Page 258

© School Zone Publishing 06338

317

ANSWER KEY

Page 261

Page 262

Page 263

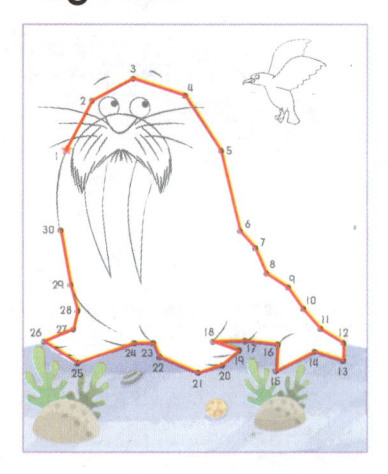

Page 264

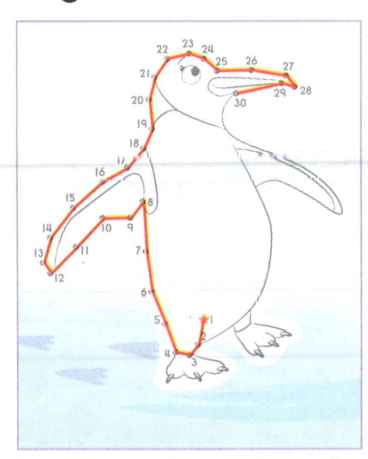

Page 265

Page 266

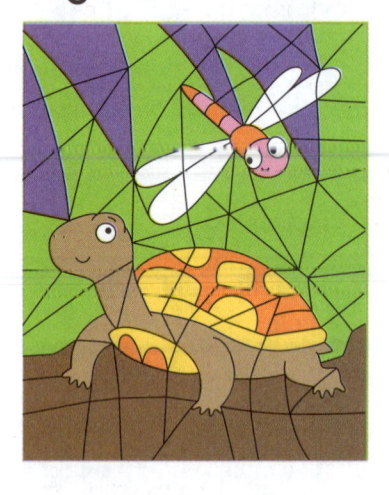

Page 269

Pages 270-271

Page 272

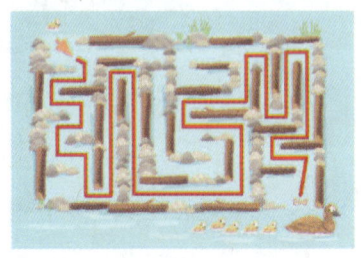

318

ANSWER KEY

Page 275

Page 276

Page 277

Page 278

Page 279

Page 280

Page 283

	1	2	3	4	5	6	7	8	9	10	11	12
Ducks	■	■	■	■	■	■						
Frogs	■	■	■	■	■	■	■	■				
Turtles	■	■	■	■	■							
Dragonflies	■	■	■	■								

Page 284

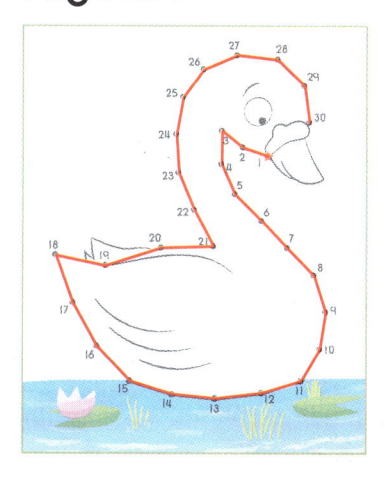

Page 285

1. s e a l
   k
   u
   n
2. k o a l 3. a
           n
           t
4. o c t o p u s

Pages 286–287

319

© School Zone Publishing 06338

ANSWER KEY

Page 288

	b	i	r	d		
				e		
				e		
	r	h	i	n	o	
					t	
					t	
		b	e	a	r	

Page 289

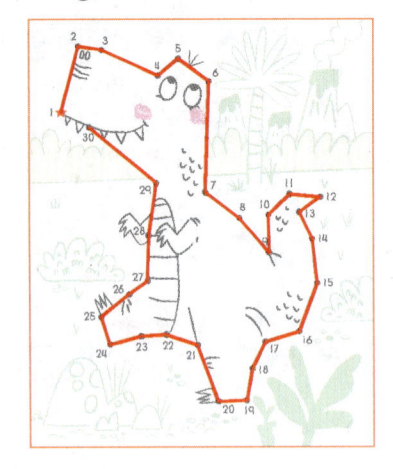

Page 290

Page 293

Page 294

Page 295

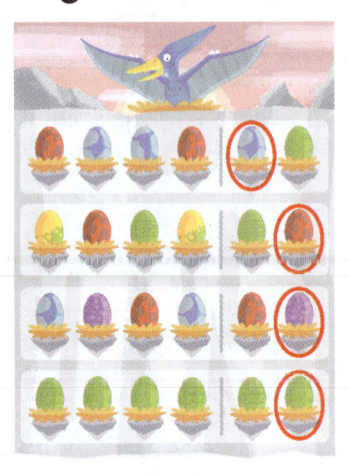

Page 296

Page 297

Page 298

320

© School Zone Publishing 06338